爆发力训练

——中英对照双语教材

黄迎乒　张振东　主编

人民体育出版社

图书在版编目（CIP）数据

爆发力训练：中英对照双语教材 / 黄迎乒, 张振东主编. -- 北京：人民体育出版社, 2020（2023.6重印）
 ISBN 978-7-5009-4150-7

Ⅰ.①爆… Ⅱ.①黄… ②张… Ⅲ.①肌肉—力量训练—教材—汉、英 Ⅳ.①G808.14

中国版本图书馆CIP数据核字(2020)第248017号

*

人民体育出版社出版发行
天津画中画印刷有限公司印刷
新 华 书 店 经 销

*

787×960　16开本　11.25印张　202千字
2020年12月第1版　2023年6月第2次印刷

*

ISBN 978-7-5009-4150-7
定价：51.00元

社址：北京市东城区体育馆路8号（天坛公园东门）
电话：67151482（发行部）　　邮编：100061
传真：67151483　　　　　　　邮购：67118491
网址：www.psphpress.com

（购买本社图书，如遇有缺损页可与邮购部联系）

编委会

主　编　　黄迎兵　张振东

副主编　　叶新江　申军辉　张海威

编　委（排名不分先后）

　　　　　张亚坤　王绥隆　张兴涵
　　　　　孙　凯　乐严严　杨　庆
　　　　　高　昊　马利强　熊一鸣　达志强

动作模特

　　　　　董姝含　高　昊

英文翻译

　　　　　聂世轩　张亚坤　王绥隆
　　　　　张兴涵　陈永欢　尚　远

内容介绍
Reminder

　　为加强普通高校大学生素质教育，有效提高大学生体育文化素养，本书在归纳、总结众多爆发力训练方法的基础上进行了创新，一是采用中英文对照的编写方法；二是针对爆发力锻炼建立起一套完整的训练体系；三是采用"爆发力练习+评价量表"训练模式。在借鉴大量文献和最新成果的基础上，全书用六章内容详细介绍了以徒手静力练习和借助杠铃、哑铃、弹力带、瑞士球等器械进行的爆发力量练习。针对不同水平、不同层次的大学生来说，本书提供了丰富的、最简单易行和最具参考意义的身体爆发力训练方法。

　　In order to strengthen the quality education of college students and effectively improve their sports and cultural literacy, this book has carried out innovation on the basis of summarizing many explosive power training methods. Firstly, it adopts the compilation method of Chinese and English; secondly, it establishes a complete training system for explosive strength training; thirdly, it adopts the training mode of "explosive power training + evaluation scale" .On the basis of a large number of references and the latest achievements, the book uses six chapters to introduce the explosive strength training with the help of barbell, dumbbell, elastic band

and swiss ball.For different levels of college students, this book provides a wealth of, the easiest to do and the most meaningful reference of physical explosive training methods.

本书在编写过程中努力实现内容丰富，材料翔实，图文并茂的目标，遵守融科学性、专业性、知识性、趣味性于一体，可读性强的编写原则，使其既可作为普通高校体育文化素质教育的教材，也可作为大学生提高自身体育文化素养的自学读物和锻炼指南。

In the process of compiling this book, we strive to achieve the principles of rich content, full and accurate materials, pictures and texts, integration of scientificity, professionalism, knowledge and interest, and strong readability, so that it can not only be used as teaching materials of physical culture quality education in colleges and universities, but also be used as self-study reading materials and exercise guide for college students to improve their own sports cultural literacy.

前 言
Foreword

随着我国素质教育的全面推行与基础教育向素质教育的全面转轨,要求当代大学生德、智、体、美、劳全面发展。一方面,大学体育是学校体育与社会体育的衔接点,是大学生健身意识、终身体育习惯和体育能力形成的关键期,校园体育文化的快速发展,学校体育的地位逐渐提高;另一方面,当代大学生身心日趋成熟,思维活跃,认知和判断能力都达到了较高水平,是接受高层次教育与实现人格社会化的最佳时期。

With the overall implementation of quality education in China and the transition from basic education to quality education, it requires the all-round development of morality, intelligence, physique, beauty and labor of contemporary college students. On the one hand, college physical education is the connection point between school physical education and social sports, and it is the critical period for the formation of College Students' fitness consciousness, lifelong sports habits and sports ability. With the rapid development of campus sports culture, the status of school sports is gradually improved; on the other hand, the physical and mental maturity of contemporary college students, active thinking, cognitive and judgment ability have reached a higher level, which is the best period to accept a high level of education and socialization of personality.

《体育强国建设纲要》提出持续提升体育发展的质量和效益，大力推动全民健身与全民健康深度融合，不断满足人民对美好生活需要的指导思想，明确坚持以人民健康为中心，制订并实施全民健身计划，普及科学健身知识和健身方法，因时因地因需开展全民健身活动的战略任务。

"Sports power construction program" puts forward the guiding ideology of continuously improving the quality and efficiency of sports development, vigorously promoting the deep integration of national fitness and national health, and constantly meeting the people's needs for a better life. It also makes it clear that people's health is the center, the whole people's fitness plan is formulated and implemented, scientific fitness knowledge and methods are popularized, and national health is carried out as the strategic task of physical activity according to the time and place.

体育文化素养是在先天遗传素质的基础上，通过后天环境与体育教育的影响所形成的，包括体质水平、体育知识、体育意识、体育行为、体育技能、体育个性、体育品德等要素的综合素质与修养。体育文化素养是大学生各种体育精神要素及其品质相结合而形成的一种体育素质。提升大学生体育素质,增进大学生健康水平,符合素质教育的时代要求,得到了我国高等教育的广泛认同和重视。

Sports cultural accomplishment is formed on the basis of congenital genetic quality and through the influence of acquired environment and physical education, including comprehensive quality and cultivation of physical fitness level, sports knowledge, sports consciousness, sports behavior, sports skills, sports personality and sports morality.Sports cultural accomplishment is a kind of sports quality formed by the combination of various sports spirit elements of college students and their qualities.To improve the physical quality of college students and improve their health level is in line with the requirements of the times of quality education, which has been widely recognized and valued by China's higher education.

大学生体育素质主要是依托高校体育教育,在促进大学生的全面发展,传授体育知识和能力,培养体育道德的教育过程中逐渐形成的,是体育锻炼和思维活动相辅相成的教育结果。体育教育是区别于大学其他学科的不同教育方式,在大学生素质教育中起到了提高身体素质与体育技术能力,并起到促进心理健康,传播体育知识与文化的重要作用。

The physical quality of college students is mainly based on Physical Education in colleges and universities. It is gradually formed in the process of promoting the all-round development of college students, imparting sports knowledge and ability, and cultivating sports morality. It is the educational result that physical exercise and thinking activities complement each other. Physical education is different from other disciplines in the university. It plays an important role in improving physical quality and sports technical ability, promoting mental health and spreading sports knowledge and culture.

高校进行体育教学的目的不仅是加强学生身体素质,更重要的是培养学生体育精神。在体育教学过程中,体育运动爆发力的训练是重要教学内容之一,爆发力是单位时间内所做的功。在进行体育运动中,爆发力是速度和力量的结合,对学生进行爆发力的训练中,可以培养创新体育能力,也能够有效地培养学生终身体育意识。爆发力也是反映高校大学生体育能力强弱的重要指标,也反映学生体育技能的客观凭证。对于高校大学生,发展体育运动爆发力是学生体育运动的基本能力,同时也是提升体育意识的重要环节。在进入大学之后,通过更加系统的体育爆发力训练,能够更好地培养学生对体育的认识,深化大学生的体育认知,并培养终身体育意识。

The purpose of physical education teaching in colleges and universities is not only to strengthen students' physical quality, but also to cultivate students' sports spirit.In the process of physical education teaching, the training of sports explosive force is one of the important teaching contents. Explosive force is the work done in unit time.In sports, explosive force is the combination of speed and strength. In the training of explosive force, students' innovative sports ability can be cultivated, and students' lifelong sports consciousness can be effectively cultivated. The explosive force is also an important index reflecting the strength of college students' sports ability and the objective evidence of students' sports skills. For college students, the development of sports explosive force is the basic ability of students' sports, but also an important link to enhance sports awareness.After entering the university, through more systematic sports explosive training, we can better cultivate students' understanding of sports, deepen college students' sports cognition, and cultivate their lifelong sports consciousness.

普通高校在体育课教学中采用"爆发力量练习+评价量表"模式，能够丰富体育课教学体系，正确评价大学生肌肉状况与爆发力量训练效果，激发大学生主动参与体育训练的兴趣，改善大学生的身体素质和运动能力，为其终身体育打下坚实的基础，增强我国国民体质健康水平。

The mode of "explosive strength training + evaluation scale" is adopted in physical education teaching in colleges and universities, which can enrich the teaching system of physical education, correctly evaluate the muscle condition and explosive strength training effect of college students, stimulate college students interest to participate in sports training actively, improve their physical quality and sports ability, lay a solid foundation for their lifelong sports, and enhance the national physical health of our country.

全书用50余种训练方法,加配高质量示范图,进行徒手动作、单一器械、复合器械,哑铃、杠铃、瑞士球等动作解析,并详细介绍了"爆发力量训练+评价量表"的使用方法。本书在编写过程中结合大学生的身体特点,从学生的兴趣入手,选取运动解剖学图谱,插入锻炼小帖士,结合评价量表,以深入浅出的语言,图文并茂的形式,由浅入深、由易到难递进式总结出不同部位爆发力量的训练方法。

More than 50 kinds of training methods and high-quality demonstration drawings are used in the book to analyze unarmed movement, single instrument, compound instrument, dumbbell, barbell, Swiss ball, etc., and the use method of "explosive strength training + evaluation scale" is introduced in detail. In the process of compiling, combined with the physical characteristics of college students, starting from the students' interests, selecting the sports anatomy atlas, inserting exercise tips, combined with the evaluation scale, summed up the training methods of explosive strength in different parts in the form of simple language and pictures, from easy to difficult.

本书在编写过程中参考和借鉴了大量文献和最新成果，特别是顾德明先生的运动解剖学图谱。本书由黄迎乒、张振东两位教授带领申军辉、高昊两位硕士研究生共同完成。参加写作团队成员（排名不分先后）：张亚坤（第一章）、王绥隆（第五章）、张兴涵（第六章）、高昊（第二章）、马利强（第四章第一、二节）、熊一鸣（第四章第三、四节）、达志强（第三章）。全书英文翻译：聂世轩、陈永欢、尚远、张兴涵、王绥隆、张亚坤，动作模特：高昊、董姝含。全书最后由黄迎乒、张振东进行统稿、校对。

In the process of compiling this book, a large number of literatures and latest achievements have been referred to, especially Mr. Gu Deming's Atlas of sports anatomy.This book is jointly completed by two postgraduates, Shen Junhui and Gao Hao, under the leadership of Professor Huang Yingping and Zhang Zhendong. Members of the writing team （regardless of rank）：Zhang Yakun（chapter 1）, Wang Suilong（chapter 5）, Zhang Xinghan（chapter 6）, Gao Hao（chapter 2）, Ma Liqiang（section 1 and section 2 of chapter 4）, Xiong Yiming（section 3 and section 4 of chapter 4）, Da Zhiqiang（chapter 3）.Translated into English：Nie Shixuan, Chen Yonghuan, Shang Yuan, Zhang Xinghan, Wang Suilong, Zhang Yakun; action models：Gao Hao, Dong Shuhan.Finally, Huang Yingping and Zhang Zhendong compiled and proofread the whole book.

本书把"中英文对照"形式和"爆发力量练习+评价量表"模式主要以创新形式写进教学内容，形成教学体系，试图推广到全国高校，达到共同提高大学生的体育文化素质与爆发力量之目的，希望对高校教师与大学生体育教学与运动训练工作能够有所启发。本书在编写过程中，还参考了大量中外学者的优质文献，在此，对于文献作者表示衷心感谢。鉴于著者水平所限，编书过程中难免存在遗漏与不足，书中若有不妥之处，敬请广大读者批评指正。

In this book, the main innovative forms of "Chinese English comparison" form and "explosive strength exercise + evaluation scale" mode are written into the teaching content, forming a teaching system, trying to popularize to the national colleges and universities, so as to jointly improve the sports cultural quality and core strength of college students, hoping to inspire the physical education teaching and sports training work of college teachers and college students. In the process of compiling this book, we also refer to a large number of high-quality literature of Chinese and foreign scholars, and once again express our heartfelt thanks to the author of the literature. In view of the limited level of the author, there are inevitably omissions and deficiencies in the process of compiling the book. If there is something wrong in the book, please criticize and correct it.

目 录
Content

绪论…………………………………………………………………（ 1 ）
Introduction………………………………………………………（ 1 ）

第一章　爆发力训练理论…………………………………（ 15 ）
Chapter 1　Theory of explosive power training………（ 15 ）

　第一节　爆发力量……………………………………………（ 15 ）
　Section 1　Explosive strength………………………………（ 15 ）

　第二节　爆发力训练…………………………………………（ 19 ）
　Section 2　Explosive power training………………………（ 19 ）

　第三节　大学生爆发力训练解析……………………………（ 22 ）
　Section 3　Analysis on the explosive power training of college students
　………………………………………………………………（ 22 ）

第二章　爆发力训练的热身和放松活动…………………（ 25 ）
Chapter 2　Explosive strength training warm-up and relaxes
　………………………………………………………………（ 25 ）

　第一节　热身活动、放松活动的理论意义…………………（ 25 ）
　Section 1　Theoretical significance of warm-up and relaxes……（ 25 ）

第二节　训练前的热身活动…………………………………（ 34 ）
Section 2　Warm-up activities before training………………（ 34 ）

第三节　训练后的放松活动…………………………………（ 44 ）
Section 3　Relaxation activities after training………………（ 44 ）

第三章　爆发力徒手训练………………………………………（ 46 ）
Chapter 3　Unarmed training of explosive power……………（ 46 ）

第一节　爆发力徒手练习的理论意义………………………（ 46 ）
Section 1　Theoretical sense of unarmed explosive power training………（ 46 ）

第二节　徒手爆发力训练方法………………………………（ 51 ）
Section 2　Unarmed explosive force training method………（ 51 ）

第四章　爆发力训练——单一器械……………………………（ 72 ）
Chapter 4　Explosive power training—single apparatus
………………………………………………………………（ 72 ）

第一节　杠铃训练方法………………………………………（ 72 ）
Section 1　Barbell training methods…………………………（ 72 ）

第二节　壶铃训练方法………………………………………（ 84 ）
Section 2　Kettlebell training methods………………………（ 84 ）

第三节　健身球训练方法……………………………………（ 89 ）
Section 3　Fitness ball training methods……………………（ 89 ）

第四节　弹力带训练方法……………………………………（ 93 ）
Section 4　Training method of resistance band……………（ 93 ）

第五节　跳跃训练方法………………………………………（118）
Section 5　Jumping training methods………………………（118）

第五章 爆发力训练复合器械
Chapter 5　Explosive strength training with instruments　(130)

第一节　杠铃类练习……………………………………………（130）
Section 1　Barbell exercises……………………………………（130）

第二节　复合器械类……………………………………………（139）
Section 2　Composite instruments……………………………（139）

第六章 爆发力训练测量与评价
Chapter 6　Explosive training measurement and evaluation　(142)

第一节　爆发力量测量与评价简介……………………………（142）
Section 1　Introduction to explosive force measurement and evaluation……………………………………………………（142）

第二节　测量与评价方法………………………………………（147）
Section 2　Measurement and evaluation methods…………（147）

后　　记……………………………………………………………（156）
Postscript…………………………………………………………（156）

绪 论
Introduction

随着经济和社会的全面发展、民众生活水平的提升,以及全球"健康推进"计划的实施,健康已然成为人类社会共同关注的焦点,成为世界各国追求富强、文明的重要内容。2016年3月17日,中共中央发布了《中华人民共和国国民经济和社会发展第十三个五年规划纲要》,提出将"健康中国"作为国家战略实施,文件中多处提及健康中国和体育的关系。2016年10月,我国颁布了《"健康中国2030"规划纲要》,第一次把"健康中国"提升为国家战略,明确了建设"健康中国"的思路与任务。在中国共产党第十九次全国代表大会报告中也提出"加快推进体育强国建设",这是第一次在党代会中明确提出建设体育强国,体育强国建设是新时期中国体育发展的主要目标和宏伟蓝图,是事关亿万中国人民全民健身和全民健康的发展战略。

With the comprehensive development of economy and society, the improvement of people's living standards, and the implementation of the global "health promotion" plan, health has become the focus of human society's common concern and has become an important part of the world's pursuit of prosperity and civilization. On March 17, 2016, the Central Committee of the Communist Party of China promulgated the "Thirteenth Five-Year Plan for National Economic and Social Development of the People's Republic of China", proposing the implementation of "Healthy China" as a national strategy. Many references to the relationships between healthy China and sports in the document. In October 2016, China promulgated the "Healthy China 2030 Plan", which promoted "Healthy China" to a national strategy for the first time and clarified the ideas and tasks for building "Healthy China". In the report of the 19th National Congress of the Communist Party of China, it also proposed to "accelerate the construction of a strong country in sports". This is the first time that the construction of a sports power is clearly put forward in the party congress. The construction of a sports power is the main goal and grand blueprint for China's sports development in the new era.

It is a development strategy that affects the fitness and national health of hundreds of millions of Chinese people.

中国青少年体质健康水平始终是国人关注的焦点，在2006年8月19日举行的"首届中国青少年体质健康论坛"上，国家教育部体育卫生与艺术教育司司长杨贵仁出示了一组数据："最近一次全国青少年体质健康调查报告表明，学生肥胖率在过去五年内迅速增加，四分之一的城市男生是'胖墩'。眼睛近视的比例，初中生接近六成，高中生为七成六，大学生高达八成三。[1]"中国男性平均身高低于日韩：世界男性平均身高排名中，韩国排第18位，平均身高1.74米；日本第29位，平均身高1.707米；中国男性排名第32位，1.697米。7~17岁的中国男孩平均身高比日本同龄男孩矮2.54厘米。从事基础教育工作的全国人大代表吴正宪2014年3月6日列举上述数据并呼吁尽快建立针对校园学生意外伤害的安全保护法规，激发学校让孩子们积极参加体育锻炼的热情，确保增强学生体质[2]。

The health status of Chinese adolescents has always been the focus of Chinese people's attention. At the "First China Youth Physical Health Forum" held on august 19, 2006, Yang Guiren, Director of the Department of Sports Health and Art Education of the Ministry of Education, presented a set of data: the latest National Adolescent Physical Health Survey report showed that the obesity rate of students has increased rapidly in the past five years, and one in four urban boys is 'fat'. The proportion of myopia in the eyes is close to 60% for junior high school students, 76% for high school students and 83% for undergraduates. The average height of Chinese males is lower than that of Japan and South Korea: The average height of men in the world ranks 18th in South Korea, with an average height of 1.74 meters; 29th in Japan, with an average height of 1.707 meters; Chinese men rank 32nd 1.697 meters. The average height of Chinese boys between the ages of 7 and 17 is 2.54 cm shorter than that of Japanese boys of the same age. Wu Zhengxian, a NPC deputy who is engaged in basic education, listed the above data on March 6, 2014 and called for the establishment of safety protection laws for accidental injuries to students

---

[1] 中国青少年体质最近20年持续下降"硬、软、笨". 中国网：http://www.china.com.cn
[2] 中国男性平均身高矮于日韩代表疾呼增强学生体质. 新华网：http://www.xinhuanet.com

on campus as soon as possible, inspiring children actively participate in physical exercise and ensure that students enhance their physical fitness.

2018年教育部体育卫生与艺术教育司司长王登峰表示："2014年全国学生体质健康调研结果显示，全国学生体质健康状况与2010年相比，部分指标有所好转，中小学生身体素质持续下滑趋势在2010年得到初步遏制后，继续呈现'稳中向好'趋势。[1]"

In 2018, Wang Dengfeng, Director of the Department of Physical Education and Art Education of the Ministry of Education, said: "The results of the 2014 National Physical Fitness Survey show that compared with 2010, some of the indicators of the national students' physical health have improved, and the physical quality of primary and secondary school students has continued to decline. After initial containment in 2010, it continues to show a trend of 'steady and good'."

2018年3月初，北京体育大学教授、运动与体质健康教育部重点实验室主任张一民针对2017年全国学生体质健康状况变化特征的抽查结果表示：受教育部体育卫生与艺术教育司委托，从2015年到2017年，对全国学生体质健康标准测试上报的数据进行抽查复核，并对当年各地各校上报的体测数据进行统计分析和结果比对，抽查对象是从小学一年级到大学四年级的学生。在对比2015年和2016年的数据后，得出结论：经过多年的努力，我国青少年的体质终于稳步回升了[2]。

At the beginning of March 2018, Zhang Yimin, professor of the Beijing Sport University and director of the Key Laboratory of the Ministry of Sports and Physical Health, said that the results of the survey on the changes in the physical health status of the national students in 2017 indicated that they were entrusted by the Department of Sports Health and Art Education of the Ministry of Education from 2015. By 2017, the data reported by the National Student Physical Health Standards Test will be checked and reviewed, and the physical analysis data and the results of the physical examinations reported by the schools

---

[1] 教育部体卫艺司党支部书记、司长王登峰：学校体育美育充分协调发展是高质量教育的标志. 中华人民共和国教育部官方网站：http://www.moe.gov.cn

[2] 艰难的反转。中华人民共和国教育部官方网站：http://www.moe.gov.cn

in each year will be compared. The students will be selected from the first grade to the fourth grade. After comparing the data of 2015 and 2016, it is concluded that after years of hard work, the physical fitness of our young people has finally steadily rebounded.

　　大学生终身体育意识，作为高校体育教学的宗旨之一，显然包括着各种运动形式的爆发力培养，由此，爆发力训练也会从细节能力上推动大学生终身体育意识的培养。大学生作为人青年时期最朝气蓬勃的阶段，除了各种创造性的精神以外，还会通过他们健康、阳光、阳刚与冲劲的外表表现出来。因而，爆发力立足他们青年时期的开始阶段，应该有着和其年龄、身心成长相当的特征体现。如速度，无论是作为高校体育考核内容之一，还是作为个人体能素质之一，都有着既定的标准，是合格、良、优秀甚或不及格等。如耐力，此项也以长跑运动作为考核形式，作为大学生基本的体育运动内容，检验着他们的健康指数。如力量，不管是长跑还是短跑，考核的都是腿部的力量，包括重点冲刺时的爆发力，当然也有单杠运动、双杠运动考核的则是双臂的爆发力等。

College students' lifelong sports consciousness, as one of the purposes of college physical education, obviously includes the cultivation of explosive power of various sports forms. Therefore, the explosive force training will also promote the cultivation of college students' lifelong sports consciousness from the perspective of detail ability. College students, as the most vigorous stage in their youth, not only have a variety of creative spirit, but also through their healthy, sunny, masculine and energetic appearance. Therefore, the explosive force is based on the beginning stage of their youth, and should have the characteristics of their age, physical and mental growth. For example, speed, whether as one of the contents of physical examination in colleges and universities, or as one of personal physical qualities, has established standards, which are qualified, good, excellent or even failed. Such as endurance, this item is also as the form of long-distance running, as the basic sports content of college students, testing their health index. For example, strength, whether it is long-distance running or sprinting, is the strength of the legs, including the explosive power of the key sprint, of course, there are horizontal bar sports, parallel bar sports, the assessment is the explosive power of both arms.

尽管大学生们的身体素质普遍不高甚至有些不达标，但是，身心成长阶段决定了他们具有青年的激情，他们也喜欢各种运动，并且希望通过一切机会来表现自己或展现自己的才能等。然而，任何具有美感的动作表演或发挥的体育项目，都需要爆发力的支持。爆发力支持他们兴趣的发挥。对于那些他们热爱的体育项目，他们身体素质可能并不足以按照一定的时间、力量等要求去完成它，但可以让他们在高频率的练习中始终保持着兴趣。

Although the physical quality of college students is generally not high, even some do not meet the standard, but the physical and mental growth stage determines that they have youth passion, they also like all kinds of sports, and hope to show themselves or show their talents through every opportunity. However, any sports with aesthetic performance or play, need the support of explosive force. Explosive power supports their interest. For those sports they love, they may not have enough physical fitness to complete it according to certain time and strength requirements, but they can get the maintenance of interest in high frequency practice.

爆发力支持他们体能极限的提升。尽管一部分大学生的体能并不理想，甚至各种考核项目都不能及格，但相对于他们自身而言也有着自己的极限，在他们具有爆发力的情况下，会带动他们在爆发中挑战自己的极限，如速度、耐力、力量等，使得他们在这种临界的发挥中，不自觉地提升自己。

Explosive power supports their physical strength to the limit. Although some college students' physical fitness is not ideal, and even all kinds of examination items can not pass, they also have their own limits relative to themselves. When they have explosive power, they will drive them to challenge their own limits in the explosion, such as speed, endurance, strength., which makes them unconsciously improve themselves in this critical play.

大学生运动爆发力是大学生体育能力的要素之一，只有在爆发力发挥的基础上，他们的体育能力才能得到技术性、技能性与专业性的展现，且能与个人实际结合起来实现个人体育方式的创新。在大学生高校学习阶段，无论是体育考核需要，还是个人体育运动需要，运动爆发力都是其日常体育运动的基础能力。在田径运动中，运动爆发力支持他们完成各种关键的冲刺使能力正常或超常发挥。如跑、跳、掷等运动形式，爆发力会让他们发挥出超常的能力来，进而取得理想的成绩，如速度的提高、投掷距离的加大、个人耐力与冲刺能力的提升等。在球类运动中，运动爆发力支持他们实现理想的拼抢与战术攻守转化。无论是篮球、足球、排球或乒乓球等运动中，运动爆发力会让他们积极地参与拼抢，并在团队或个人危机的时刻迸发出超越自己的体能素质来，如篮球的精彩篮板球、足球的抢断、乒乓球的回击、排球的扣杀等，最终让自己转危为安，或持续保持对抗优势。在体操与舞蹈类运动中，运动爆发力支持他们去完成理想中的高难度美感动作。不管是体育舞蹈、健美操或其他的舞蹈运动，那些具有震撼力、感染力等特征的优美动作，都与爆发力有关。在运动者爆发力的支持下，他们才能把相应的技巧技能按照自己的理解尽情地发挥出来，如舞蹈中的旋、腾、跳及其相互结合的动作完成等。

College students' sports explosive power is one of the elements of college students' sports ability. Only on the basis of exerting the explosive force, can their sports ability be shown in terms of technology, skill and specialty, and can be combined with personal reality to realize the innovation of individual sports mode. In the stage of college students' study in colleges and universities, whether it is the need of physical examination or individual sports needs, sports explosive power is the basic ability of their daily sports. In track and field, the explosive force of sports supports them to complete all kinds of critical sprints and normal or extraordinary performance of their ability. Such as running, jumping, throwing and other forms of sports, explosive force will let them play their extraordinary ability, and then achieve ideal results, such as the improvement of speed, the increase of throwing distance, the improvement of personal endurance and sprint ability. In ball games their attack and defense tactics are transformed into sports support. Whether it is basketball, football, volleyball, table tennis or other sports, the explosive power of sports will make them actively participate in the fight, and burst out to exceed their own physical quality at the time of team or personal crisis, such as the wonderful bank ball of basketball, the interception of football, the return stroke of table tennis, the smash of volleyball, and so on, so that they can turn the crisis into safety, or maintain the advantage of confrontation. In gymnastics and dance sports, the explosive force of sports supports them to complete the ideal and difficult aesthetic movement. Whether it is sports dance, aerobics or other dance sports, those beautiful movements with the characteristics of shock and appeal are related to explosive force. With the support of athletes' explosive force, they can give full play to the corresponding skills and skills according to their own understanding, such as the dance of spin, Teng, jump and their combination of action completion.

无论是体育专业的大学生,还是非体育专业的大学生,他们在立足自己专业知识的基础上,结合个人的体育运动需要、身体体能实际以及个性化发展需要等,都会按照自己的需要去创新属于自己的个性运动形式。这些个性化的体育锻炼方式,都必须立足在他们自身运动爆发力的基础上,进而按照个人体能成长规律,去实现循序渐进的体质成长。

Whether they are sports majors or non sports majors, based on their own professional knowledge, combined with personal sports needs, physical fitness and personality development needs, they will innovate their own individual sports forms according to their own needs. These personalized physical training methods must be based on their own sports explosive force, and then according to the law of individual human body growth, to achieve gradual physical growth.

本书从提高大学生体育文化素养角度,结合高校大学生爆发力量训练的现状,从不同训练方法的新视角,系统阐述爆发力量的科学化训练依据,论述爆发力量训练的概念,制订出实施爆发力量训练的运动处方,归纳大学生体质健康测试的评价量表,旨在进一步讨论爆发力量训练对高校大学生身体素质的影响,探究能有效提升高校体育教学质量与高校大学生体育素质的有效途径。

From the perspective of improving college students' sports cultural literacy, combining with the current situation of college students' explosive strength training, from a new perspective of different training methods, this book systematically expounds the scientific training basis of explosive strength, discusses the concept of explosive strength training, formulates the exercise prescription for implementing explosive strength training, and summarizes the evaluation scale of college students' physical health test, aiming at further discussion. This book discusses the influence of explosive strength training on the physical quality of college students, and explores the effective ways to effectively improve the quality of college physical education and college students' physical quality.

人体骨骼-肌肉群示例
Examples of human skeletal muscle groups

肌肉结构
Muscle structure

人体大约有639块肌肉，这些肌肉由60亿条肌纤维组成，其中最长的肌纤维达60厘米，最短的仅有1毫米左右。大块肌肉约有两千克重，小块的肌肉仅有几克。一般来说，人的肌肉占体重的35%~45%。

There are about 639 human muscles. It is composed of about 6 billion muscle fibers, of which the longest is 60 cm and the shortest is only about 1 mm. Large muscles weigh about two thousand grams, and small muscles weigh only a few grams. General, person's muscle accounts for about 35 to 45 percent of body weight.

人体肌肉按结构和功能的不同可分为平滑肌、心肌和骨骼肌三种，按形态又可分为长肌、短肌、阔肌和轮匝肌。平滑肌主要构成内脏和血管，具有收缩缓慢、持久、不易疲劳等特点。心肌构成心壁，两者都不随人的意志收缩，故称不随意肌。骨骼肌分布于头、颈、躯干和四肢，通常附着于骨，骨骼肌收缩迅速、有力、容易疲劳，可随人的意志舒缩，故称随意肌。骨骼肌在显微镜下观察呈横纹状，故又称横纹肌。

According to the structure and function, muscles can be divided into smooth muscle, myocardium and skeletal muscle. According to the shape, it can be divided into long muscle, short muscle, broad muscle and orbicularis muscle. Smooth muscle is mainly composed of viscera and blood vessels, with slow contraction, long-lasting, not easy to fatigue and other characteristics, the heart constitutes the heart wall, both do not contract with the will of people, so it is called involuntary muscle. Skeletal muscle distributed in the head, neck, trunk and limbs, usually attached to bone, skeletal muscle contraction is rapid, powerful, easy to fatigue, can be relaxed and contraction with the will of people, so it is called voluntary muscle. Skeletal muscle is striated under microscope, so it is also called striated muscle.

骨骼肌是运动系统的动力部分,分为白、红肌纤维,白肌依靠快速化学反应迅速收缩或者拉伸,红肌则依靠持续供氧运动。在神经系统的支配下,骨骼肌收缩,可牵引骨产生运动。人体骨骼肌共有600余块,分布广,约占体重的40%,每块骨骼肌不论大小如何,都具有一定的形态、结构、位置和辅助装置,并有丰富的血管和淋巴管分布,受一定的神经支配。因此,每块骨骼肌都可以看作是一个器官。

Skeletal muscle is the dynamic part of the exercise system, which is divided into white and red muscle fibers. White muscle contracts or stretches rapidly by rapid chemical reaction, while red muscle relies on continuous oxygen supply. Under the control of the nervous system, skeletal muscle contraction, traction bone movement. There are more than 600 skeletal muscles in human body, which are widely distributed, accounting for about 40% of the body weight. No matter how big or small, each skeletal muscle has a certain shape, structure, location and auxiliary devices. It also has rich blood vessels and lymphatic vessels and is controlled by certain nerves. Therefore, each skeletal muscle can be regarded as an organ.

头肌可分为面肌(表情肌)和咀嚼肌两部分。躯干肌可分为背肌、胸肌、腹肌和膈肌。下肢肌按所在部位分为髋(kuan)肌、大腿肌、小腿肌和足肌,均比上肢肌粗壮,这与支持体重、维持直立及行走有关。上肢肌按所在部位分为:肩肌、臂肌、前臂肌、手肌、颈肌。

The head muscle can be divided into facial muscle (facial muscle) and masticatory muscle. The trunk muscle can be divided into dorsal muscle, chest muscle, abdominal muscle and diaphragm. The lower limb muscles are divided into hip muscle, thigh muscle, calf muscle and foot muscle according to their location, which are thicker than the upper limb muscle, which is related to supporting weight, maintaining upright and walking. Upper limb muscles are divided into shoulder muscle, arm muscle, forearm muscle, hand muscle and neck muscle.

肌肉分类
Muscle classification

骨骼肌: 是可以看到和感觉到的肌肉类型。当健身者通过锻炼增加肌肉力量时，锻炼的就是骨骼肌。骨骼肌附着在骨骼上且成对出现：一块肌肉朝一个方向移动骨头，另外一块朝相反方向移动骨头。这些肌肉通常随意志收缩，意味着想要收缩它们时，神经系统会指示它们这样做。骨骼肌可以做短暂单次收缩（颤搐）或长期持续收缩（破伤风）。

Skeletal muscle: the type of muscle that can be seen and felt. When a gymnast increases muscle strength through exercise, it's skeletal muscle. Skeletal muscles are attached to bones and appear in pairs: one muscle moves the bone in one direction and the other moves the bone in the opposite direction. These muscles usually contract with the will, which means that when they want to contract them, the nervous system instructs them to do so. Skeletal muscles can be contracted for a short time (twitching) or long-term continuous contraction (tetanus).

红、白肌纤维：人体的骨骼肌可以分为红肌和白肌两种纤维。红肌纤维依靠血红蛋白持续供氧运动，进行较长时间的收缩和拉伸，从而使我们进行日常行为活动。而白肌纤维则（多在紧急情况下）依靠内部快速化学反应迅速伸缩，其特点是持续、反应时间短，其反应时间是红肌纤维的四分之一。

Red and white muscle fiber: human skeletal muscle can be divided into red muscle and white muscle fiber. Red muscle fiber relies on hemoglobin for continuous oxygen supply exercise, for a long time of contraction and stretching, so that we can carry out daily activities. However, white muscle fibers (mostly in emergency situations) rely on internal rapid chemical reaction to expand and expand rapidly, which is characterized by continuous and short reaction time, and its reaction time is one fourth of that of red muscle fibers.

平滑肌：存在于消化系统、血管、膀胱、呼吸道和女性的子宫中。平滑肌能够长时间拉紧和维持张力。这种肌肉不随意志收缩，意味着神经系统会自动控制它们，而无需人去考虑。例如，胃和肠中的肌肉每天都在执行任务，但人们一般都不会察觉到。

Smooth muscle: present in digestive system, blood vessel, bladder, respiratory tract and womb. Smooth muscle can stretch and maintain tension for a long time. The muscles don't contract with the will, which means that the nervous system controls them automatically without human consideration. For example, muscles in the stomach and intestines perform tasks every day, but people generally don't notice.

心肌：只存在于心脏，它最大的特征是耐力和坚固。它可以像平滑肌那样有限地伸展，也可以用像骨骼肌那样的力量来收缩。它只是一种颤搐肌肉并且不随意志收缩。心肌有固定的收缩规律从而产生心跳，正常人的起搏细胞正常，心肌收缩规律一定。起搏细胞出现异常，心肌收缩规律则会发生改变。

Heart muscle: only exists in the heart, its biggest characteristic is endurance and firmness. It can stretch as limited as a smooth muscle, or it can contract with the strength of a skeletal muscle. It's just a twitching muscle that doesn't contract with the will. The heart muscle has a fixed contraction law, which produces a heartbeat. In normal people, the pacemaker cells are normal, and the law of myocardial contraction is certain. If the pacemaker cells are abnormal, the law of myocardial contraction will be changed.

肌肉构造
Muscle structure

组成运动器官的每一块肌肉都是一个复杂的器官，由肌腹和肌腱两部分组成。肌腹是肌器官的主要部分，位于肌器官的中间，由许多骨骼肌纤维借助结缔组织结合而成，具有收缩能力，包在整块肌肉外表面的结缔组织称为肌外膜。肌外膜向内伸入，把肌纤维分成大小不同的肌束，称为肌束膜。肌束膜再向内伸入，包围着每一条肌纤维，称为肌内膜。肌膜是肌肉的支持组织，使肌肉具有一定的形状。血管、淋巴管和神经随着肌膜进入肌肉内对肌肉的代谢和机能调节具有重要作用。

Every muscle that constitutes the motor organ is a complex organ, which is composed of two parts: muscle belly and tendon. Muscle belly is the main part of muscle organs, located in the middle of muscle organs, by many skeletal muscle fibers combined with connective tissue. With the ability to contract, the connective tissue wrapped in the outer surface of the whole muscle is called the adventitia. The adventitia extends inward, dividing the muscle fibers into muscle bundles of different sizes, known as the myofascial membrane, and then extends inward, surrounding each muscle fiber, known as the intramuscular membrane. The muscle membrane is the supporting tissue of muscle, which makes the muscle have a certain shape. Blood vessels, lymphatic vessels and nerves enter the muscle along with the muscle membrane, which plays an important role in the regulation of muscle metabolism and function.

肌腱位于肌腹的两端，由致密结缔组织构成。肌腱在四肢多呈索状，在躯干多呈薄板状，又称腱膜。腱纤维借肌内膜连接肌纤维的两端或贯穿于肌腹中。肌腱不能收缩，但有很强的韧性和张力，故而不易疲劳。肌纤维伸入骨膜和骨质中，使肌肉牢固地附着于骨上。

The tendon is located at both ends of the muscle belly and is composed of dense connective tissue. The tendon are mostly cord like in the limbs, in the trunk are mostly thin plate, also known as aponeurosis. The tendon fiber connects the two ends of muscle fiber or runs through the muscle abdomen through the muscle intima. The tendon can not contract, but it has strong toughness and tension, so it is not easy to fatigue. The muscle fibers extend into the periosteum and bone, making the muscle firmly attached to the bone.

肌肉的构造为：肌肉→肌束→肌纤维（肌细胞）→肌原纤维→肌节（肌动蛋白、肌球蛋白）。

The structure of muscle is: muscle → muscle bundle → muscle fiber (muscle cell) → myofibril → sarcomere (actin, myosin).

如果我们像一个细胞那么小，能够随意进入人的身体，那么当我们来到肌肉群中时，就会发现肌肉是由一道道钢缆一样的肌纤维捆扎起来的。这些钢缆组合成较粗较长的缆绳群组，当肌肉用力时，它们就像弹簧一样一张一缩。在那些最粗的缆索之内，有肌纤维、神经、血管，以及结缔组织。每根肌纤维是由较小的肌原纤维组成的。每根肌原纤维，则由缠在一起的两种丝状蛋白质（肌凝蛋白和肌动蛋白）组成。这就是肌肉的最基本单位，全是由这两种小得根本无法想象的蛋白组合成的，当它们联合起来以后，就能做出人的各种动作来。

If we are as small as a cell and can enter the human body at will, then when we come to the muscle group, we will find that the muscle is bound by a series of steel cable like muscle fibers. These cables are combined into groups of thicker and longer cables, and when muscles exert force, they stretch and contract like springs. Within the thickest cables are muscle fibers, nerves, blood vessels, and connective tissue. Each muscle fiber is composed of smaller myofibrils. Each myofibril is composed of two filamentous proteins (myosin and actin) that are intertwined. This is the basic unit of muscle, which is made up of these two incredibly small proteins, and when combined, they can make any kind of movements.

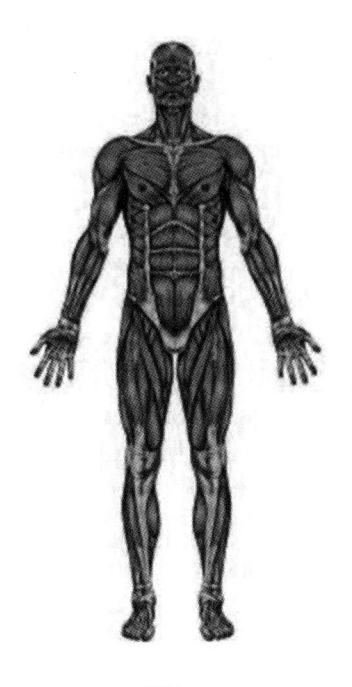

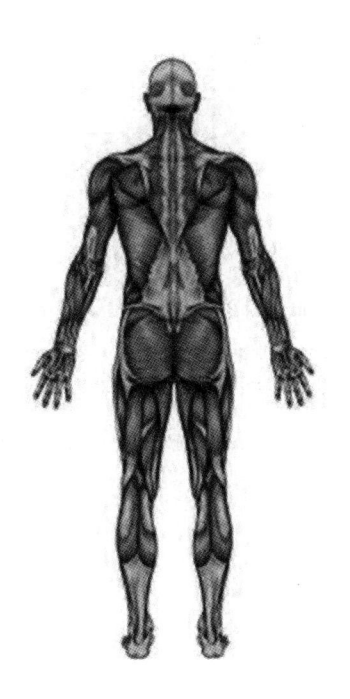

图1

图2

图 3

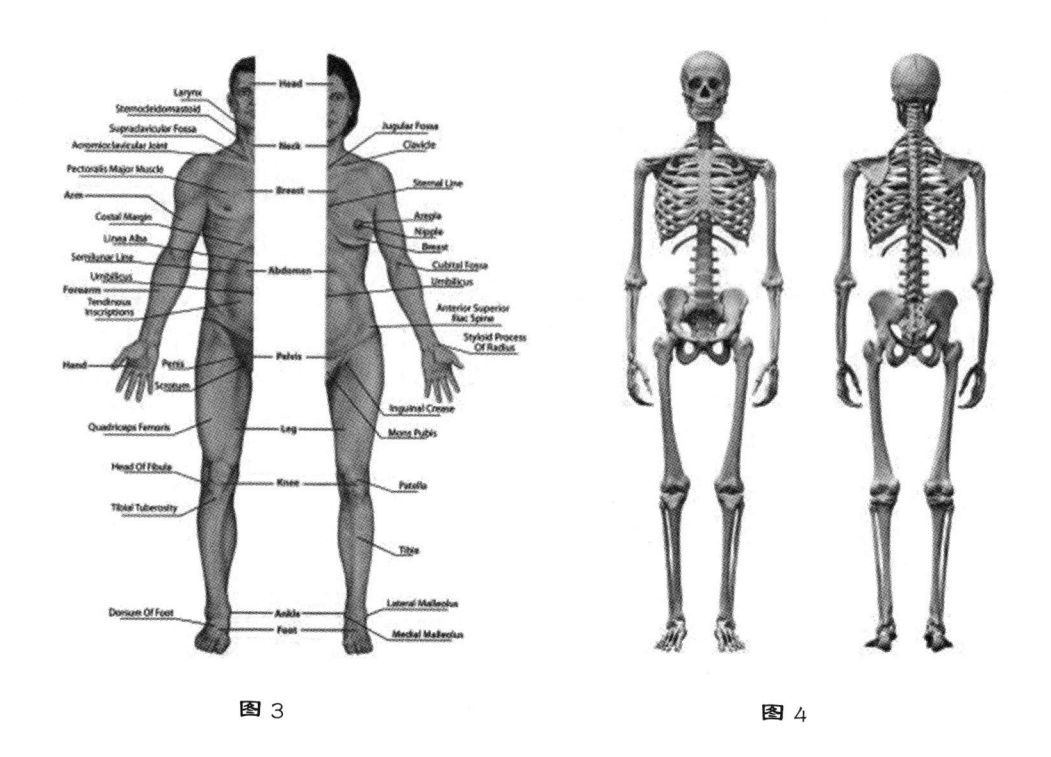

图 4

随着人们年龄的不断增长，控制骨头活动的横纹肌的弹性纤维会逐渐由结缔组织所代替。结缔组织虽然很结实，但没有弹性，因此肌肉变得较弱，不能强力收缩。所以老年时，肌肉的力量衰退，反应也迟钝了。人老了，肌肉的力量也就衰弱了。

As people grow older, the elastic fibers of the striated muscles that control bone activity are gradually replaced by connective tissue. Although the connective tissue is very strong, it has no elasticity, so the muscles become weak and cannot be strongly contracted. So in old age, the muscles strength will declines and their response will be slow. As you get older, the strength of your muscles get weaker.

第一章　爆发力训练理论
Chapter 1　Theory of explosive power training

第一节　爆发力量
Section 1　Explosive strength

1　爆发力
1　Explosive power

爆发力在很多运动项目尤其是举重、球类、短跑等项目中都扮演着举足轻重的角色。随着运动技术的不断提高，爆发力与最终的运动成绩有着越来越密切的关系，所以深受教练员和广大研究学者的重视。

Explosive power plays an important role in many sports, especially in weightlifting, ball games and sprint. With the continuous improvement of sports technology, the explosive power has a more and more close relationship with the final sports performance, so that it is deeply valued by coaches and researchers.

目前人们对爆发力的应用关注很多，但对爆发力这个概念本身却缺乏理论的共识，并且对爆发力有着不同的理解和定义。通过对此问题进行讨论，试图引起人们对爆发力的探讨，最终找到解决问题的方案或达成某种一致的看法。

At present, people pay much attention to the application of explosive power, but there is lack of theoretical consensus on the concept. There are different understandings and definitions of explosive power. By discussing this problem, we try to arouse people's discussion on explosive power, and finally find a solution to the problem or reach some consensus.

2 爆发力的定义
2 Definition of explosive power

金子出宥认为:"在最大努力的基础条件下,能保证最短时间内产生强大机械功率的肌肉活动能力,就是爆发力。"

Jinzi Chuyu believes that: "under the basic conditions of best efforts, the muscle activity ability that can ensure the generation of strong mechanical power in the shortest time is the explosive power."

苏联学者库兹涅夫认为:"爆发力是指肌肉在克服极限阻力过程中产生最大加速度的能力。"我国学者王清认为:"从训练实践角度上看,宏观把爆发力看作是肌肉在极短的时间内通过迅速而强有力的收缩产生最大的加速度去克服的能力。"爆发力最终目的是在最短时间内使器械(或人体本身)移动到尽量远的距离,是不同的肌肉间相互协调能力,力量素质以及速度素质相结合的一项人体体能素质。可以说爆发力就是肌肉克服负荷量和收缩距离时,在最短时间内能产生的最大肌张力。

Kuznev, a former Soviet scholar, said: "explosive strength refers to the ability of muscle to produce maximum acceleration in the process of overcoming the ultimate resistance." Wang Qing, a Chinese scholar, believes that: "from the perspective of training practice, the macro view of explosive strength is the ability of muscles produce the maximum acceleration through rapid and powerful contraction in a very short period of time to overcome resistance." The ultimate purpose of explosive power is to make the equipment (or the human body) move as far as possible in the shortest time. It is a human physical quality which combines the coordination ability of different muscles, strength quality and speed quality. It can be said that explosive power is the maximum muscular tension that can be produced in the shortest time when the muscle overcomes the load and contraction distance.

3 爆发力的影响因素
3 Influencing factors of explosive power

根据运动生理学、生物力学的原理,在相同用力距离下,爆发力的大小取决于肌肉收缩力量和速度的最佳组合。在运动技术中,通常把力和速度的乘积 $P=FV$ 称为爆发力,因此功率又被称为肌肉收缩的爆发能力。

According to the principles of sports physiology and biomechanics, under the same force distance, the explosive power depends on the best combination of muscle contraction strength and speed. In sports technology, the product of force and velocity $P=FV$ is usually called explosive power, and so that power is also called explosive ability of muscle contraction.

3.1 肌肉收缩力量大小的影响因素
3.1 Influencing factors of muscle contraction strength

肌肉力量的大小与很多生理因素有关。主要的因素有:

Muscle strength is related to many physiological factors. The main factors are as follows:

① 肌肉的生理横断面。肌肉生理横断面增大是由于肌纤维增粗造成的,而肌纤维的增粗则主要是收缩性蛋白质含量的增加,负重肌肉力量练习对增大肌肉生理横断面有良好效果。

① physiological cross section of muscle. The enlargement of physiological cross section of muscle is caused by the thickening of muscle fiber, while the thickening of muscle fiber is mainly due to the increase of contractile protein content. Weight bearing muscle strength training has a good effect on increasing muscle physiological cross section.

② 肌群的协调能力。在现实生活中,常可见到两个人肌肉粗细程度相似,但两人力量并不相同,这就是肌肉中肌纤维的动员程度及各肌群之间的协调能力的差异。

② The coordination ability of muscle groups. In real life, we can often see that the muscle thickness of two people is similar, but their strength is not the same, which is the difference of the mobilization degree of muscle fibers in muscles and the coordination ability between muscle groups.

3.2 影响速度能力的因素
3.2 Factors affecting speed capability

神经系统的工作状态是影响速度能力的重要因素之一,神经系统在有机体整体工作时可以影响运动员参与工作的注意力集中程度,这就直接影响运动员完成技术动作的好坏,它也直接影响肌肉紧张的程度。

速度能力的表现水平与肌组织的最佳状态有关,在放松时肌弹性最小,紧张时肌弹性最大,肌肉的放松能力越高,肌肉的紧张度越高,它们之间的交替状态越协调,则速度能力的表现水平也越高。

The working state of the nervous system is one of the important factors that affect the speed ability. When the whole organism works, the nervous system can affect the concentration of athletes participating in the work, which directly affects the performance of athletes' technical actions and the degree of muscle tension.

The performance level of speed ability is related to the best state of muscle tissue. The muscle elasticity is the smallest when relaxing, and the maximum is when the muscle is tense. The higher relaxation ability of muscle is, the higher tension of muscle is. The more harmonious the alternate state between them is, the higher performance level of speed ability is.

4 爆发力发展水平
4 Explosive power development level

在大多数运动项目中,爆发力的发展水平是制约和决定动作速度和移动速度的重要因素之一。在大多数运动项目的比赛中,不仅要求运动员必须具备快速完成动作的技能,还要求以同样的形式长时间多次重复动作的能力。因此,在速度训练中,提高爆发力必须与提高肌肉耐力同时进行,只有这样才有助于长时间快速工作的能力。

In most sports, the development level of explosive power is one of the important factors that restrict and determine the movement speed and movement speed. In most sports competitions, athletes are required not only to have the skills to quickly complete the movements, but also to repeat the movements repeatedly for a long time in the same form. Therefore, in the speed training, the improvement of explosive power must be carried out at the same time as the improvement of muscle endurance. Only in this way can the ability of long-term and fast work be improved.

第二节　爆发力训练
Section 2　Explosive power training

1　爆发力训练的概述
1　An overview of explosive power training

速度是爆发力的一个重要因素。在做爆发力训练的时候一定有时间参数，并且要关注动作轨迹的速度，有些快速收缩类训练并不是爆发力训练。爆发力训练要尽量保证训练的安全，有些快速收缩类动作重复的时候身体并没有做好准备，没有用到肌肉牵张反射，而是不得不进行时，很容易导致伤病，这类训练不是爆发力训练。

Speed is an important factor in explosive power. When doing explosive power training, there must be a time parameter. We should pay attention to the speed of the movement track. Some fast contraction training is not explosive power training. Explosive power training must be as safe as possible. When some fast contraction movements are repeated, the body is not ready and does not use muscle stretch reflex, but has to be carried out. This can easily lead to injury, this kind of training is not explosive training.

2　爆发力训练的原则
2　Principles of explosive power training

效率原则：爆发力训练必须设法以最少的人力、物力、财力与时间达到最大的训练效果。

Efficiency principle: explosive power training must try to achieve the maximum training effect with the least manpower, material resources, financial resources and time.

特殊原则：爆发力训练必须符合该项运动之特性。

Special principle: explosive training must conform to the characteristics of the sport.

持续原则：训练期间必须持之有恒，不得间断。

The principle of continuity: during the training period, it must be persistent and uninterrupted.

变动原则：长期变动原则。

Principle of change: long term change principle.

第一阶段：无负荷跳跃训练。

The first stage: no load jumping training.

第二阶段：轻负荷跳跃训练。

The second stage: light load jumping training.

第三阶段：重负荷跳跃训练。

The third stage: heavy load jumping training.

第四阶段：伸展收缩训练。

The fourth stage: stretching and contraction training.

短期变动原则：

Short term change principle:

训练方式之变化

changes in training methods

训练其强度之变化

the change of training intensity

训练速度之变化

the change of training speed

3 爆发力训练的功能与作用
3 The functions of explosive power training

爆发力是指单位时间内所做的功，在实际的运动中，代表着速度与力量的结合。

Explosive power refers to the work done in unit time. In actual motion, it represents the combination of speed and strength.

3.1 爆发力训练增强身体肌肉
3.1 Explosive power training strengthens body muscles

许多练举重的朋友为了长更多的肌肉，因此不断挑战愈大的负重，但若搭配爆发力的训练,能获得更多神经肌肉的控制及唤醒更多的肌群,更助于力量的增加。

In order to gain more muscles, many weightlifters constantly challenge the heavier load. However, if combined with explosive power training, more neuromuscular control can be obtained and more muscle groups can be recruited, which will help to increase strength.

3.2 爆发力训练改善关节控制能力
3.2 Explosive power training to improve joint control

在进行杠铃深蹲时,你没办法控制膝盖或髋关节的动作,你就不能够增加更多的负重在杠铃上。研究指出,在15周肌肉爆发力的训练中,15周结束之后,发力率明显的改善了,更重要的是,肌肉的关节控制方式改变了,神经肌肉、关节控制及稳定度也都提升了。而有好的关节稳定度意味着你可以举起更高的负重。

In a barbell squat, you can't control the movement of your knees or hips, then you can't add more weight to the barbell. The study points out that in the 15 week training of muscle explosive power, at the end of 15 weeks, the rate of power output has been significantly improved. More importantly, the joint control mode of muscles has changed, and the neuromuscular, joint control and stability have also been improved. Good joint stability means you can lift higher loads.

3.3 爆发力训练延长寿命
3.3 Explosive power training prolongs life

随着年纪的增加,我们的平衡感及其他功能因神经连接与反应时间的递减而功能受损。研究指出,爆发力训练比起肌力训练更能改善老年人口的生理功能,爆发力训练能改善日常生活的功能及延长寿命。

As we get older, our sense of balance and other functions are impaired by the decline of nerve connections and reaction time. Studies have shown that explosive power training can improve the physiological function of the elderly population more than muscle strength training, and explosive strength training can improve the daily life function and prolong life span.

第三节 大学生爆发力训练解析

Section 3 Analysis on the explosive power training of college students

1985年至2005年，五次大规模中国学生体质与健康调研显示，中国青少年学生在身体形态、生理功能和身体素质多个指标上呈现出不同程度的水平下降现象，部分指标的下降倾向呈加速趋势。《分析报告》显示，2008年以来，学生体质健康下降趋势得到一定程度遏制，但整体上反映出来的指标值仍然令人担忧，特别是在以下指标上，显现的问题十分突出。

From 1985 to 2005, five large-scale surveys of Chinese students' physique and health showed that Chinese young students' body shape, physiological function and physical fitness showed different degrees of decline, and some indicators turned out to be an accelerated trend. "Analysis report" shows that since 2008, the declining trend of students' physical health has been curbed to a certain extent, but the overall index value reflected is still worrying, especially in the following indicators, the problems are very prominent.

1 肺功能指标维持低水平
1 Lung function index maintained low level

肺活量/体重指数可以在一定程度上反映人的肺功能。《体质调研》显示，1985—2005年，肺活量和肺活量/体重指数在20年间总体呈下降趋势。《分析报告》显示，2008年学生的肺活量/体重指数分布，优秀率为15.62%，良好率为22.59%，及格率为39.24%，不及格率为22.54%。2010年各年龄组测试结果与2008年相比，整体水平略有提高，不及格率降至20.08%，但是，肺功能总体水平仍然处于较低水平。

Lung capacity / body mass index can reflect the lung function to some extent. According to the "physical survey", lung capacity and vital capacity / body mass index showed a downward trend in the 20 years from 1985 to 2005. According to the analysis report, the excellent rate of students in 2008 was 15.62%, the good rate was 22.59%, the passing rate was 39.24%, and the failure rate was 22.54%. Compared with 2008, the overall level of the test results of all age groups in 2010 increased slightly, and the failure rate dropped to 20.08%. However, the overall level of lung function is still at a low level.

2 速度、力量素质增长趋于停滞
2 The growth of speed, strength quality tends to be stagnant

速度、爆发力、力量素质是人体运动能力的重要基础。《体质调研》显示，1995—2005年，学生身体素质中反应速度素质的50米跑成绩、反应爆发力素质的立定跳远成绩和反应力量素质的引体向上、斜身引体、仰卧起坐成绩，除速度素质下降幅度较小外，其他素质均有明显下降。

Speed, explosive power and strength quality are the important foundation of human movement ability. Physical fitness survey shows that from 1995 to 2005, except for the speed quality, the speed quality of the 50 meter running performance, the standing long jump performance of the explosive power quality and the pull-up, oblique body pull-up and sit up results of the reaction strength quality, except the speed quality decreased slightly, the other qualities decreased significantly.

3 柔韧素质与关节周围韧带、肌腱、肌肉等软组织的伸展性数据
3 Flexibility and extensional data of ligaments, tendons and muscles around joints

通过测试坐位体前屈成绩，反映人体的柔韧素质。《分析报告》显示，2008年，学生总体坐位体前屈的优秀率为27.75%，及格以上比率为97.31%；2010年，学生总体坐位体前屈的优秀率为28.21%，及格以上比率为97.40%。不同学段学生坐位体前屈比较表明，其优秀率以大学最好，其次为小学和初中，最次为高中。2008—2010年，各学段学生及格以上比率均在96%以上，是学生所有素质中成绩最好的指标。

By testing the performance of sitting body forward flexion, it reflects the flexibility of human body. According to the analysis report, in 2008, the excellent rate of sitting forward flexion was 27.75%, and the pass rate was 97.31%; in 2010, the excellent rate of sitting forward flexion was 28.21%, and the pass rate was 97.40%. The comparison of students in different periods showed that the excellent rate of college students was the best, followed by primary school and junior high school, and the last was senior high school. From 2008 to 2010, more than 96% of the students passed the examination, which is the best indicator of all the qualities of students.

4 超重和肥胖现象严重
4 Overweight and obesity are serious

《分析报告》显示，2008年学生不同营养状况检出率营养不良占8.58%，低体重占42.21%，标准体重占37.01%，超重占4.55%，肥胖占7.66%。2018年统计显示，超重和肥胖分别增加到5.05%和9.41%，表明由营养过剩导致的肥胖和超重情况继续恶化。

According to the analysis report, in 2008, the malnutrition rate of students with different nutritional status accounted for 8.58%, low weight accounted for 42.21%, standard weight accounted for 37.01%, overweight accounted for 4.55%, and obesity accounted for 7.66%. In 2018, the statistics showed that overweight and obesity increased to 5.05% and 9.41% respectively, indicating that the situation of obesity and overweight caused by excessive nutrition continued to worsen.

所有运动都离不开爆发力，无论是足球、篮球、短跑等各项运动，爆发力永远占主要位置。只要同学们的爆发力强，基础打得好，运动水平就会得到很大的提升。

All sports are inseparable from explosive power, whether it is football, basketball, sprint and other sports, explosive power will always occupy the main position. As long as the students' explosive power is strong and the foundation is good, the sports level will be greatly improved.

发展青少年爆发力的方法有很多，但由于青少年训练的特殊性，需要在训练的方法和手段上更加符合青少年的特点，在训练中应选择那些比较安全而且有效的方法和手段以发展他们的爆发力，才能达到良好的效果。

There are many ways to develop teenagers' explosive power. However, due to the particularity of teenagers' training, the training methods and means should be more in line with the characteristics of teenagers. In order to achieve good results, we should choose safe and effective methods and means to develop their explosive power.

第二章 爆发力训练的热身和放松活动

Chapter 2　Explosive strength training warm-up and relaxes

第一节　热身活动、放松活动的理论意义

Section 1　Theoretical significance of warm-up and relaxes

1　热身活动解析
1　Analysis of warm-up activities

热身活动，具体是指运动员为训练或比赛所进行的前奏活动，是运动训练和比赛中一个极其重要的基础环节。积极的热身活动可以提高训练水平，为比赛取得好成绩创造条件，同时，还可以积极预防运动损伤的发生。

Warm-up activities, specifically referring to the prelude activities performed by athletes for training or competition, are an extremely important basic link in sports training and competition. Active warm-up activities can improve the level of training and create conditions for good results in the competition. At the same time, it can also actively prevent sports injuries.

运动热身是任何运动训练的重要组成部分，热身的重要性在于可以避免运动损伤的发生。减少损伤的风险系数。一个有效的热身包含很多重要的元素，这些组成的元素共同作用才使得运动的损伤风险降到最低。热身是身体活动之前进行的运动，有很多的益处，热身的首要作用是让身心做好准备接受艰苦的训练。帮助身体增加身体的核心温度，肌肉温度。肌肉温度的增加可以使肌肉更松弛，更灵活。有

效的热身可以增加心率次数和呼吸的深度与频率。增加血液流量、血液氧气和血液中营养供给肌肉，帮助肌肉的肌腱与关节接受更多的训练。

Warm up is an important part of any sports training. The importance of warm-up is to avoid sports injury. Reduce the risk factor of damage. An effective warm-up contains many important elements, which work together to minimize the risk of injury. Warm up is a kind of exercise before physical activity, which has many benefits. The primary function of warm-up is to prepare the body and mind for hard training. Help the body increase the body's core temperature and muscle temperature. The increase of muscle temperature can make the muscle more relaxed and flexible. An effective warm-up can increase heart rate and the depth and frequency of breathing. Increase of blood flow, blood oxygen and blood nutrients to the muscles, help muscle tendons and joints receive more training.

首先，热身是简单和轻松动作开始，循序渐进地让身体接受更高强度的训练，促进身体和心理到达巅峰状态，最大限度地降低身体遭遇运动损伤的风险，因此，每个运动的人都应该把热身纳入自己实行目标的一个重要部分。完整的热身活动应该包括：一般热身、静止肌肉拉伸、运动专项的热身和动态的肌肉拉伸。这四个部分都是重要的，任何其中的一个部分都是不可以忽略。四个部分联合作用给身体和心理的积极影响，从而使运动员的身体进入巅峰状态。

First of all, warm-up is the beginning of simple and easy movements, it will gradually let the body accept higher intensity of training, promote the physical and mental to reach the peak state, as far as possible to reduce the risk of physical injury. Therefore, every sports person should have warm-up as an important part of their implementation goals. Complete warm-up should include: general warm-up; static muscle stretching; sports specific warm-up and dynamic muscle stretching. These four parts are important, and any one of them can not be ignored. The combined effect of the four parts has a positive impact on the body and psychology, so that the athlete's body can enter into the peak state.

国内外对热身活动的研究表明，热身活动能使运动员充分调动人体各系统的活力，能打破运动员的各种生理惰性。另外，良好的热身活动能使运动员的中枢神经系统兴奋起来，从而能更大限度地调动运动系统的积极性，为取得优异成绩提供保证。

Research on warm-up activities in China and abroad shows that warm-up activities can make athletes fully mobilize the vitality of various systems of the human body and break the various physiological inertia of athletes. In addition, a good warm-up can excite the athlete's central nervous system, which can mobilize the enthusiasm of the sports system to a greater extent and provide a guarantee for achieving excellent results.

热身运动中加入核心激活练习有助于提高运动员的最大力量和爆发力。在训练和竞赛前要进行充分而良好的热身活动，可使肌肉的温度及肌键韧带的温度升高，降低肌肉的黏滞性，增加肌肉伸展性及弹性，使其柔韧性延展性加强，扩大其活动范围的效果，为取得好的运动成绩及预防运动损伤提供积极的可能性。

Adding core activation exercises to the warm-up exercise helps improve the athlete's maximum strength and explosive power. Perform adequate and good warm-up activities before training and competitions, which can increase the temperature of the muscles and the muscle bond ligaments, reduce the viscosity of the muscles, increase the stretchability and elasticity of the muscles, and strengthen the flexibility and expansion. The effect of its range of activities provides positive possibilities for achieving good sports performance and preventing sports injuries.

在进行热身活动时，牵拉运动是不可缺少的重要组成部分，应该引起足够的重视，使热身活动的效果更合理、更充分。

Stretching exercise is an indispensable and important part of warm-up activities. It should attract enough attention to make the effect of warm-up activities more reasonable and full.

2 放松活动解析
2 Analysis of relaxation activities

放松训练指的是使机体从紧张状态松弛下来的一种练习过程。放松训练的直接目的是使肌肉放松，最终目的是使整个机体活动水平降低，达到心理上的松弛，从而使机体保持内环境平衡与稳定。放松训练的形式多种多样，有渐进式放松训练、印度的瑜伽术、日本的禅宗，以及中国的气功。放松训练的基本要求是：在安静的环境下，练习者要做到心情安定，注意力集中，肌肉放松。在做法上要注意循序渐进，放松训练的速度要缓慢。对身体某部分肌肉进行放松时，一定要留有充分时间，以便让被试者细心体会当时的放松感觉。放松训练能否成功，决定于被试者对此项训练的相信程度，是否密切配合。放松成功的标志是，各肌肉均处于松弛状态，肢体和颈部张力减低，呼吸变慢。受训练者若处于仰卧位置，则出现足外展。

Relaxation training refers to a kind of exercise process that makes the organism relax from the tense state. The direct purpose of relaxation training is to relax the muscles, and the ultimate goal is to lower the activity level of the whole body and achieve psychological relaxation, so as to keep the balance and stability of the internal environment. There are various forms of relaxation training, including progressive relaxation training, yoga in India, Zen in Japan and Qigong in China. The basic requirements of relaxation training are: in a quiet environment, practitioners should be in a stable mood, pay attention to concentration and relax muscles. In practice, we should pay attention to step by step, and the speed of relaxation training should be slow. When relaxing a certain part of the body muscles, it is necessary to leave enough time for the subjects to carefully experience the feeling of relaxation at that time. Whether the relaxation training is successful or not depends on the degree of confidence and close cooperation of the subjects. Successful relaxation is marked by the relaxation of muscles, decreased tension in the limbs and neck, and slow breathing. If the trainees are in the supine position, they will have foot abduction.

肌肉主动性放松。训练课后，安排强度在50%~55%的长距离慢跑，学生普遍感到疲劳恢复的很快。这是因为机体疲劳过程中如果采用积极的恢复手段，如低强度慢跑，耐力跑等有助于加快血液循环，挤压血液向上回流。而且血液循环的加快有助于乳酸的排斥使学生的心肺功能逐渐恢复到安静状态，有利于学生的健康。慢跑的方式不仅能够达到身体放松的目的，而且可以起到调节心理的作用。在慢跑时应该注意的是，不要使身体过多地出汗，以避免过度地消耗体力。

The muscles actively relax. After the training session, arrange a long-distance jogging with an intensity of 50%~55%. The students generally feel fatigue and recover quickly. This is because active recovery methods such as low-intensity jogging and endurance running can help accelerate blood circulation and squeeze the blood back upwards. Moreover, the acceleration of blood circulation helps the rejection of lactic acid and gradually restores the cardiopulmonary function of the students to a quiet state, which is beneficial to the health of the students. The way of jogging can not only achieve the purpose of physical relaxation, but also can regulate the mind. What should be noted when jogging is not to make the body sweat too much to avoid excessive physical exertion.

肌肉被动牵拉性放松。运动后及时做一些拉长肌肉韧带的静力牵拉练习，能促进肌肉的乳酸代谢，以缓解肌肉和关节的酸痛感觉，促进肌肉疲劳的恢复，减少再次运动时由于肌肉没有恢复而造成的伤害。一般来说，运动过程中或运动后都应注意放松整理活动。牵拉肌肉的时间应该选择在慢跑结束后进行。散打专项训练后，包括前臂肌的屈伸牵拉、肘关节的牵拉、肩关节内收牵拉、肩关节上举牵拉、腰背肌腹肌牵位、大腿屈伸肌的牵拉。上述六种牵拉方法，可根据参与活动的肌肉疲劳感做不同的练习。应该遵循循序渐进的原则，开始时用力小一些，动作的幅度也相对小一些，然后逐渐加大用力和动作的幅度。牵拉背部和臀部肌肉时最好采用体前屈和下蹲屈体团身的姿势。牵拉大腿后群肌肉时也是采用体前屈的动作，但膝关节应该微屈，这样效果更好一些。在牵拉大腿前群肌肉时可以双膝跪在垫子上，然后慢慢向后倒体。在牵拉小腿后群肌肉时，要采用屈膝体前屈，一腿前伸勾脚尖，重心放在后腿上的姿势，左右交替进行。

The muscles relax passively. Do some static stretching exercises to lengthen the muscles and ligaments in time after exercise, which can promote the metabolism of lactic acid in the muscles, so as to relieve the soreness of the muscles and joints, promote the recovery of muscle fatigue, and reduce the damage caused by the muscles not recovering when exercising again. Generally speaking, attention should be paid to relaxation and tidying activities during or after exercise. The time to stretch the muscles should be selected after the end of jogging. After the special training of Sanda, it includes the flexion and extension of the forearm muscles, the stretching of the elbow joint, the adduction and stretching of the shoulder joint, the lifting and stretching of the shoulder joint, and the back muscle abdominal muscle traction, traction of thigh flexor and extensor muscles. The above-mentioned stretching methods can be used for different exercises according to the fatigue of the muscles involved in the activity. You should follow the principle of gradual and orderly progress. At the beginning, you should use less force and the range of movement is relatively small; then gradually increase the range of force and movement. When pulling back and buttocks muscles, it is best to use forward and squat body postures. When stretching the back muscles of the thighs, the body is also flexed forward, but the knee joint should be slightly flexed for better results. When pulling the front thigh muscles, you can kneel on the mat, and then slowly fall back. When pulling the back muscles of the calf, you should bend your knees forward, stretch your toes forward with one leg, and place your weight on your hind legs, alternating left and right. Muscle massage to relax.

肌肉按摩放松。按摩放松法手法主要有按、摩、揉捏、推压、拍打等。按摩肌肉可以反射性地改善和调节中枢神经系统的机能，消除疲劳，改善肌肉的血液循环，使肌肉组织得到充分供氧，改善肌肉的代谢，并使其得到充分的放松。许多部位学生可以自己按摩放松，自己按摩不到的部位可相互进行按摩，控制整理活动强度的目的。在放松大腿前群肌肉时，学生应该坐在垫子上，膝关节下要垫着运动服或其他的东西。在放松臀部、大腿后群和小腿后群肌肉时，学生应该俯卧在垫子上，小腿下部或脚背要垫着运动服或其他的东西。也可以俯卧在垫子上，让同伴一手扶起你的小腿，用另一手来放松按摩臀部、大腿后群和小腿后群的肌肉。此外，还可以让学生俯卧在垫子上，小腿下部或脚背要垫着运动服或其他的东西，同伴两手扶墙站在被放松学生的臀部和大腿后部、用脚进行踩压放松。

Relaxation by muscle massage. Massage and relaxation techniques mainly include pressing, rubbing, kneading, pressing and patting. To massage the muscles can reflexively improve and regulate the function of the central nervous system and eliminate fatigue; improve the blood circulation of the muscles, so that the muscle tissue can be fully oxygenated, and the muscle metabolism can be improved, and it can be fully relaxed. Students can massage many parts by themselves to relax, and the parts that cannot be massaged by themselves can massage each other to control the intensity of activities. When relaxing the front muscles of the thighs, students should sit on a mat with a cushion under the knee joint sportswear or other things. When relaxing the muscles of the buttocks, the back of the thighs and the back of the calf, students should lie prone on the mat, and the lower part of the calf or instep should be cushioned with sportswear or other things. You can also lie on your stomach on the mat, let your partner lift your calf with one hand and use the other to relax and massage the muscles of the buttocks, the back of the thigh and the back of the calf. In addition, students can also lie prone on a mat, with sportswear or other stuff on the lower leg or instep, and the companion stands on the wall of the relaxed student's hips and thighs with his feet to relax.

心理放松。心理放松法是指教学训练中教师采用愉悦的教学语言、轻松的教学训练态度和活泼的教学训练形式,使学生队员注意放松身心,沉浸在心情舒畅的情绪之中,并以"心放"来诱导身松。

Psychological relaxation. Psychological relaxation means that teachers use pleasant teaching language, relaxed teaching and training attitudes, and lively teaching and training forms in teaching and training, so that student team members can pay attention to relax their minds, immerse themselves in comfortable emotions, and "rest at ease". Inducing body loose.

放松整理活动质量如何,直接关系到运动水平的提高和教学信息及时反馈,以及运动员的身体、心理的健康发展。训练后进行放松活动,是为了解决训练中身心活动的张弛矛盾,求得二者的统一,使运动后的呼吸系统,心血管系统及肌肉、关节、韧带等在运动后得到松弛与养息,从而及时解除训练动中所形成的身体紧张状态。

The quality of relaxation activities is directly related to the improvement of exercise level and timely feedback of teaching information, as well as the healthy development of athletes' physical and mental health. Relaxation activities after training are to resolve the tension between physical and mental activities during training and seek the unity of the two, so that the respiratory system, cardiovascular system and muscles, joints, ligaments, etc. can relax and nourish after exercise, so as to relieve the body tension formed in the training exercise in time.

消除乳酸缓解疲劳,提高机体的工作能力。机体在运动中要消耗大量的能量物质,在缺氧情况下进行运动时肌肉中的糖原难以完全氧化释放能量,这就造成体内乳酸堆积。当乳酸在身体血液和肌肉中堆积超过肌体耐受限度时,就会使大脑的兴奋性降低,机体工作能力下降,学生感到疲劳,肌肉酸痛发沉。通过一系列的放松整理活动对提高消除乳酸，促进其氧化或再合成糖原有很大的功效。对缓解疲劳，提高运动机能具有重要作用。

Eliminate lactic acid to relieve fatigue and improve the body's working ability. The body consumes a large amount of energy substances during exercise. When exercising under hypoxia, the glycogen in the muscles is difficult to completely oxidize and release energy, which causes the accumulation of lactic acid in the body. When lactic acid accumulates in the body's blood and muscles to exceed the body's tolerance limit, it will reduce the excitability of the brain and the body's working ability. The students will feel tired and the muscles will become sore. Through a series of relaxation activities, it has a great effect on improving the elimination of lactic acid and promoting its oxidation or re-synthesis of glycogen. It plays an important role in relieving fatigue and improving sports performance.

偿还氧债，提高呼吸系统的机能。这样在运动以后内脏器官是继续进行高强度工作，以补偿运动时缺少的氧气。如果不做放松整理活动而直接停止运动，那么，身体的相对静止状态首光就妨碍了强烈的呼吸动作，影响氧气的补充。而适当的放松整理活动，在其中进行调整呼吸和做一些深呼吸练习，一方面可以增加吸氧量加强气体交换，偿还氧债，另一方面可以提高肺部收缩与扩张能力，有利于呼吸系统机能的提高。

Repay the oxygen debt and improve the function of the respiratory system.Inthis way,the internal organs continue to perform high-intensity work after exercise to compensate for the lack of oxygen during exercise. If you stop exercising without doing relaxing and tidying activities, the first light of the body's relatively static state will hinder strong breathing and affect oxygen supplementation. Appropriate relaxation and tidying activities, which include adjusting breathing and doing some deep breathing exercises, on the one hand can increase oxygen intake to strengthen gas exchange and repay oxygen debt, on the other hand, it can improve lung contraction and expansion capacity, which is beneficial to respiratory system function Improvement.

调节神经系统的协调性，提高神经系统的机能。大运动量后，由于体内各物质失去平衡，会发生一些变化，当运动达到疲惫状态时，血糖减少，因而使中枢神经疲劳，引起神经紊乱。此时，如能及时进行放松整理活动，会促进大脑皮层兴奋、抑制的转换，消除因疲劳引起的神经调节紊乱，调节神经系统的协调性，使神经系统的机能得到发展和提高。

Adjust the coordination of the nervous system and improve the function of the nervous system. After a large amount of exercise, due to the imbalance of various substances in the body, some changes occur in the substances in the body. When the exercise reaches a state of fatigue, the blood sugar decreases, which makes the central nervous system fatigue and causes neurological disorders. At this time, if you can perform relaxation activities in time, it will promote the excitement and inhibition of the cerebral cortex, eliminate the neuromodulation disorder caused by fatigue, adjust the coordination of the nervous system, and make the function of the nervous system develop and improve.

第二节 训练前的热身活动
Section 2 Warm-up activities before training

1 热身练习动作演示
1 Demonstration of warm-up exercises

热身时主要几处应该被拉伸的肌肉：大腿后部、大腿内侧、小腿和背部。

The main muscles that should be stretched during a warm-up: The back of the thighs, the inside of the thighs, the calves and the back.

拉伸大腿后部肌肉：站在地上，右腿伸直，左腿弯曲，外侧贴近地面，与右腿组成三角形，背部挺直，从胯部开始前倾，双手抓住右脚脚尖，保持这个姿势30秒，手触脚尖时不允许有弹动式动作（触不到脚尖也没关系）。换腿做，每条腿拉伸3~5次。

Stretch the muscles in the back of the thigh: Stand on the floor with your right leg straight your left leg bent, and the outside side is close to the ground, forming a triangle with your right leg, your back is straight, lean forward from the hip, hold the tip of your right foot with both hands, hold this position for 30 seconds, no springy movements are allowed when your hands touch the tip of your foot (it doesn't matter if you don't touch the tip). Do this on different legs, stretching each leg 3 to 5 times.

图2-2-1 **拉伸大腿后部肌肉**

拉伸大腿内侧肌肉：坐姿，双脚脚底在身前相互贴紧，膝盖向外撑并尽量靠近地面，双手抓住双脚踝，保持这个姿势，数10秒，放松，然后重复3~5次。

Stretch your inner thighs: Sit with the soles of your feet close to each other in front of you, knees out and as close as possible to the floor, hold both ankles in your hands, count to 10 seconds, relax, and repeat 3 to 5 times.

图2-2-2 拉伸大腿内侧肌肉

拉伸大腿内侧肌肉：坐姿，双脚在体前伸直并分开，保持背部和膝盖部挺直，从胯部向前屈体，双手从腿内侧去抓住双脚的脚踝，保持这个姿势，感觉大腿内侧被拉紧，放松，然后重复3~5次。

Stretch your inner thighs: Sit with your feet straight and apart in front of your body, keeping your back and knees straight, bend forward from your hips, and grab the ankles of your legs with your hands from the inside of your legs. Hold the position, feel the inside of your thighs tight and relaxed, then repeat 3 to 5 times.

图2-2-3 拉伸大腿内侧肌肉

拉伸小腿（后部）肌肉：俯身，用双臂和一条腿（伸直，脚尖着地）支撑身体，另一条腿屈于体前放松，身体重心集中于支撑脚的脚尖处，脚跟向后、向下用力，感觉到小腿后部肌肉被拉紧，保持紧张状态，数10秒，放松，重复3次，然后换另一条腿做3次。

Stretching the calf muscles (rear): Bent over, with both arms and a leg (straight, toes touchdown) to support the body, the other legs bowed to begin to relax, body centre of gravity is focused on supporting the foot toe, heel backward and downward pressure, feel calf back muscles are tensed, keep the tension, the number 10 seconds, relax and repeat 3 times, then change the other leg made 3 times.

图2-2-4　拉伸小腿（后部）肌肉

肱三头肌拉伸练习：站势，一只手臂弯曲放在头部后侧，另一侧的手握住手臂的肘关节，向相反的方向施加力量，保持动作20~30秒，然后交替进行。

Triceps stretching exercise: Standing position, one arm bent on the back of the head, the other hand holding the elbow joint of arm, applying force in the opposite direction, holding the movement for 20 seconds to 30 seconds, and then alternately.

摆胯及绕胯练习：直立，双腿分开略比肩宽，双腿微屈，手放在胯骨上。上身正直，利用腰胯力量使胯部左右摆动各10次，注意腹部收紧。然后顺时针逆时针环绕各10圈。

图2-2-5　肱三头肌拉伸练习

Crotch and crosswise: Stand erect, legs slightly wider than shoulder, legs slightly bent, hands on hipbones. The upper part of the body is straight. Use the waist and hip strength to make the hip swing from side to side for 10 times each, pay attention to the abdominal tightening. Then go clockwise and counterclockwise 10 times.

扭膝旋转练习：两腿并拢，屈膝半蹲，两手扶膝，轻轻转动膝部，可以先从左至右转动，再从右至左转动，各自转动或交替转动10~15次。
Twist knee rotation exercise: Stand with two legs together, bend knee half squat, with two hands put on knee, gently rotate knee, first from left to right rotation, and then from right to left rotation, make rotation or alternate rotation for 10-15 times.

脚尖环绕练习：直立，抬起右脚离地15厘米左右，脚跟固定脚尖画圈，顺时针逆时针各10圈。而后换左脚。
Tiptoc circling exercise: Stand upright, lift your right foot about 15cm from the ground, set your heel in a circle, clockwise and counterclockwise 10 times each. Then change your left foot.

敏捷梯：是脚步练习的主要教具，对身体的灵活性、平衡性和协调性都有所锻炼，经常练习可以增强脚底肌肉、踝关节和膝关节的小肌肉群功能；同时对很多项需要脚步快速移动的运动项目，诸如足球、篮球等都有很大的帮助。
Speed ladder: The agility ladder is the main teaching tool for footstep exercises. It exercises the flexibility, balance and coordination of the body. Regular exercise can enhance the function of the sole muscles, the small muscle groups of the ankle and knee joints; and at the same time, footsteps exercise are of great help for many fast foot moving sports such as football and basketball.

"小步前进式"训练方法：前脚掌着地，每步落在小方格以内，要求轻快、节奏感强，脚踝有弹性。

"Small step forward" training method: Touch the forefoot on the ground, with each step falls within a small square, requiring briskness, strong rhythm, and elastic ankle.

训练量

Training volume

6-9岁：共2组，组间间歇1分钟。

6-9 years old children: 2 groups in total, with 1 minute interval between groups.

10-14岁：共3组，组间间歇1分钟。

10-14 years old children: 3 groups in total, with 1 minute interval between groups.

益处：培养青少年的节奏感，增强脚踝小肌肉群力量。

Benefits: Cultivate the rhythm of young children and enhance the strength of small ankle muscles.

注意事项：如没有敏捷梯或者场地不合适，也可在家里地板或瓷砖做标记练习，但需要穿上运动鞋才可以训练。

Warm tip: If there is no agility ladder or the venue is not suitable, you can also do marking exercises on the floor or tiles at home, but you must wear sports shoes for the training.

"并步小跳接小碎步"训练方法：先连续五个并步小跳，再接小碎步跑。

"Simultaneously skipping small steps" training method: First five consecutive small jumps, and then a small break run.

益处：可以提高膝关节、脚踝小肌肉的控制能力。

Benefits: It can improve the control ability of the small muscles of the knee and ankle.

"跳箱子/台阶"训练方法：找一只足够结实的箱子或台阶，其高度要达到极限屈膝跳且能保证安全的程度。箱子前方拉一根绳，双腿越过绳点位置后迅速跳至箱子上面，屈髋屈膝，然后走下箱子，完成第二次越绳动作。在保证安全的情况下试图每组增加一点箱子或绳子的高度。

"Jump Box/Stairs" training method: Find a box or step that is strong enough, and its height must reach the limit of knee flexion and safety. Pull a rope in front of the box, jump over the rope and quickly jump to the top of the box, bend your hips and knees, and then walk off the box to complete the second rope crossing action. Try to increase the height of the box or rope a little bit for each group for ensuring safety.

"跳远"：跳远训练是发展水平爆发力和臀部运动能力的好动作。

"Long jump": Long jump training is a good movement to develop horizontal explosive power and hip movement ability.

跳跃训练中有三个重要步骤：蓄势准备，跳跃，落地。

Training method: There are three important steps in jump training: get ready, jump, and land.

蓄势准备：双脚与肩等宽呈准备姿态。然后摆动双臂，同时臀部和膝盖弯曲，在腿上加满能量。

Preparing for momentum: The feet are shoulder-width in a prepared posture. Then swing your arms while bending your hips and knees to make your legs fall with energy.

跳跃：准备好之后开始起跳，起跳同时挥动手臂，伸髋伸膝向前爆发跳出（注意：在向前跳的同时增加一个垂直向上的跳跃有助于减少膝盖落地的剪切力）。

Jump: Start to jump when you are ready, and wave your arms while jumping, extend hips and knees and burst forward (Note: Adding a vertical jump while jumping forward will help reduce the shear force of the knee landing).

落地：脚跟落地过渡，同时臀部向后屈髋屈膝顺势深蹲作为缓冲，注意保持膝盖和脚尖同一方向，控制好冲力不要太过往前。

Landing: Transition from the heel to the ground, and at the same time bend the hips backwards, bend the hips and squat homeopathically as a buffer. Keep your knees and toes in the same direction, and control the momentum not to go too far.

2 短跑热身激活操
2 Sprint warm-up activation exercise

这个训练方法是经过许多专业队的教练，进行培训交流时得出的一种训练手段。这个激活操是在垫子上进行的。花费时间大约为20分钟，有队员反映这一套做下来全身的肌肉都被激活了，非常有效果。动作有：单腿平板支撑、单腿平板支撑抬腿、侧平板支撑、侧平板支撑抬腿、侧支撑提膝、仰卧抬腿进阶、仰卧倒蹬车、仰卧前后大摆腿、仰卧左右交叉摆腿、背向四足撑、仰卧两头起、仰卧两头起进阶、俯卧跪姿举臀抬腿、跪姿提拉、跪姿后提拉和跪姿侧摆腿。这个激活操是先从腰腹力量做起，其次是背肌，最后是臀部的激活，一侧动作做完之后再换另外一条腿。这些动作也可以根据实际情况进行变动，只要能够激活到相应的肌群就可以。这个热身操能最大限度地激活肌肉来进行热身。并且能够激活一些深层肌肉和小肌肉群，能够起到很好的热身效果。慢跑和一定强度的跑虽然能够起到很好的效果，但是时代在与时俱进，热身动作不可能是一成不变的。

This training method is a training method that has been obtained through training and exchanges with coaches of many professional teams. This activation exercise is performed on the mat. It took about 20 minutes. Some team members responded that the muscles of the whole body were activated after this set of exercise was done, which was very effective. Actions include: single-leg plank support, single-leg plank support leg lift, side plank support, side plank support leg lift, side support knee lift, supine leg lift advanced, supine reverse pedal, supine front and rear swing legs, supine left and right cross Leg swing, back to four-legged support, supine with both ends up, supine with both ends up advanced, prone kneeling posture with hips and legs raised, kneeling posture lifting, kneeling posture lifting, kneeling side swinging legs. This activation exercise starts with the strength of the waist and abdomen, followed by the back muscles, and finally the activation of the buttocks. After one side is done, change the other leg. These actions can also be changed according to the actual situation, as long as the corresponding muscle groups can be activated. This warm-up exercise can maximize the activation of muscles to warm up. And can activate some deep muscles and small muscle groups, which can play a very good warm-up effect. Although jogging and running at a certain intensity can achieve good results, the times are advancing with the times, and in innovation, warm-up movements cannot remain unchanged.

3 柔韧力量操
3 Flexibility exercise

柔韧力量操是由很多动作组合起来的，是在行进间进行的，一个动作30米做完之后加速跑20米，接着重复进行，做两组。它是一种全新的训练模式，循环的训练方法，在次数、组数和组织安排的变化上具有灵活性，可以看作是一种更全面的身体训练。在训练中可以通过循环训练法来提高人的身体素质，主要表现在柔韧性和有氧耐力方面。并且减少身体发生损伤的系数，增强协调能力，增强力量，强化意志力和自信心。在训练之前应该进行系统化和专业化的课时安排计划。柔韧力量操中的动作如：手腕脚踝的放松、弓步压腿、侧压腿、俯身摸地、压脚跟、单腿俯卧撑加抱膝跳、俯身分腿跳、深蹲提膝、俯身登山和半蹲左右移动等。这些训练动作不仅能够增强心肺功能和肌肉耐力，还能够有效地提高我们身体的控制能力，使身体更加的协调。在每次的训练过程中全身的肌肉都参与进来，能够使训练更上一层楼，为取得好成绩打下基础。

Flexibility strength exercise is a combination of many movements, which are carried out during the march. After one movement is completed for 30 meters, the acceleration runs for 20 meters, and then repeats, doing two sets. It is a brand new training mode, a cyclic training method. It has flexibility in the number of times and the number of groups and changes in organizational arrangements, which can be regarded as a more comprehensive physical training. In training, a person's physical fitness can be improved through circuit training, which is mainly manifested inflexibility and aerobic endurance. And reduce the coefficient of physical damage, enhance coordination, enhance strength, strengthen willpower and self-confidence. Before training, a systematic and professional class schedule should be planned. Flexibility exercises include: relaxation of wrists and ankles, lunges and leg presses, side presses, bent over and touch the ground, heel presses, single-leg push-ups and tuck jumps, bent-leg jumps, squats and knee lifts Body climbing, squatting left and right. These training actions can not only enhance cardiorespiratory function and muscle endurance, but also effectively improve our body's control ability and make the body more coordinated. The muscles of the whole body are involved in each training process, which can take the training to a higher level and lay the foundation for good results.

4 垫上灵敏协调
4 Sensitive coordination on the mat

垫上灵敏协调是在垫子上做的一些准备活动,有前滚翻、后滚翻、虫拱、蜘蛛爬、蜥蜴爬和侧手翻等。垫上灵敏练习最直接的好处就是可以全面发展身体的协调性。在训练中,协调对成绩的发展起着非常重要的作用。协调有一部分是由遗传决定的,而且运动员在进行动作训练时,心理的疏导也是很关键的,因为有些运动员可能害怕,克服不了心理障碍。所以,进行身体的协调训练是很重要的。前滚翻和后滚翻可能听起来比较容易,但是在训练队中有很多运动员还是不会做,做得不太规范,最基础的也是最重要的,所以也是不能被忽视的。蜘蛛爬行是根据蜘蛛的爬行动作演变而来的,蜘蛛爬行能够调动身体背部的肌肉,而且能增强上肢的固定支撑能力。由于蜘蛛爬行时手臂位于身体的后面,所以对肩胛骨也能形成一定的刺激。蜥蜴爬行的特征在于前进过程中身体位置较低、宛如蜥蜴。

Sensitive coordination on the mat is some preparatory activities done on the mat, including forward roll, backward roll, insect arch, spider crawl, lizard crawl, cartwheel and so on. The most direct benefit of sensitive exercises on the mat is that it can fully develop the coordination of the body. In training, coordination plays a very important role in the development of performance. Partly determined by genetics, and when athletes are performing exercise training, psychological guidance is also very important, because some athletes may be afraid and cannot overcome psychological obstacles. Therefore, it is very important to carry out physical coordination training. Forward and backward rolls may sound easier, but there are many athletes in the training team who still can't do it. They do not do it well. The most basic is most important, so they cannot be ignored. Spider crawling is based on spiders. The crawling action evolved, spider crawling can mobilize the muscles of the back of the body, and the fixed support ability of the upper limbs. Since the arm is behind the body when the spider crawls, it can also stimulate the shoulder blades. Lizard crawling is characterized by its low body position during its advancement, like a lizard.

　　侧手翻是双手双脚同时运动,它对身体的控制能力要求较高。有一定的运动基础后,还可以作进阶的单手侧手翻。灵敏素质是各项身体素质和运动技能的综合表现。

　　Rollover is the movement of both hands and feet at the same time. It needs of higher requirements for body control. After got a certain exercise foundation, you can also perform advanced one-handed rollover. Sensitivity is the comprehensive performance of various physical fitness and sports skills.

第三节 训练后的放松活动
Section 3　Relaxation activities after training

1　放松弹性跑

1　Relaxation run

站立式起跑40~60米，要求运动员动作放松，足前掌着地，富有弹性但步子不宜过大，主要减轻踝关节的缓冲。

Standing starting run 40-60m, athletes are required to relax and with the forefoot to touch the ground, which is flexible but with steps not too big. It mainly relaxes the cushion of the ankle joint.

2　跟随跑

2　Follow and run

在训练者前面安排一领跑者领着跑。训练时，要求领跑者按规定速度领跑，而跟随者不能超越领跑者。具体方法是选择某一距离或者将不同距离合为一组。进行重复练习，也可采用变速跑形式。其重复组述、间歇时间、练习强度根据运动员能力而定。

Arrange a leader in front of the trainer to lead the run. During training, the leader is required to lead at a prescribed speed, and the follower cannot surpass the leader. The specific method is to select a certain distance or combine different distances into a group. For repeated exercises, variable speed running can also be used. The repetition, interval time, and exercise intensity are determined by the athlete's ability.

3 特殊地段跑
3 Special location running

小步跑接加速跑主要练习脚着地,提高脚的力量,体会髋膝踝的放松。高抬腿跑转入加速跑后做自然放松跑,距离20~30米。平时要多做摆臂技术练习,要求以上臂带动小臂摆动,手腕放松,不要紧握拳和耸起双肩,不要引起脖颈及面部肌肉的不必要紧张。

Carry out various running specialized exercises on the lakeside, riverside, and woods, and experience the ability to relax running. Mini-step running and accelerating running mainly practice foot landing, improve foot strength, and experience the relaxation of hips, knees and ankles. High-leg run After turning to accelerated running, do a natural relaxation run, for a distance of 20–30m. It usually needs to do more arm swing technique exercises, requiring the upper arm to drive the forearm to swing, the wrists to relax, do not clenched fists and shrug shoulders, do not cause unnecessary tension in the neck and facial muscles.

4 波浪跑
4 Wave run

在田径场两边直道上各设一起点,要求运动员加速快跑。30米后做20~30米的放松惯性跑,再转入慢跑至第二个直道的相应位置,再做同样距离快跑、惯性跑和慢跑,慢跑时间要求30~40秒,练习次数可根据运动员的训练水平的不同要求而定。此方法不仅可培养运动员的放松能力与速度感,而且对提高速度耐力也有良好的效果。

Set a point on each straight track on both sides of the track and field to require athletes to run with acceleration. After 30m, do a relaxed inertia run of 20–30m, then switch to jog to the corresponding position of the second straight, and then do the same distance fast running, inertial run and jogging, the jogging time requires 30–40s, the number of exercises may be determined on the base of the different requirements for the athlete's training level. This method can not only cultivate athletes' relaxation ability and sense of speed, but also has a good effect on improving their speed endurance.

第三章 爆发力徒手训练

Chapter 3　Unarmed training of explosive power

第一节　爆发力徒手练习的理论意义

Section 1　Theoretical sense of unarmed explosive power training

1　超等长训练法

1　Plyometric training method

超等长训练法是当前运动员爆发力训练中比较常用的一种有效训练方法，该方法在应用过程中能够有效提高运动员的下肢神经—肌肉系统的力量和灵敏性，对于提高运动员下肢爆发力有着十分有效的效果。超等长肌肉力量训练指的是对肌肉进行快速动力性负荷牵拉，使其在该过程中产生爆发性的肌肉收缩，在训练的过程中，教师会让学生通过一系列的动作，使肌肉被迫迅速进行离心收缩，紧接着转为向心收缩，如此循环往复，使下肢肌肉不断进行收缩。这种超等长训练主要以各种跳跃练习为主，在该过程中，学生不仅能够提高肌肉的爆发力，还能够有效增强起跳动作的协调性，增加下肢肌肉的反应速度和力量。在运用超等长练习时我们应注意合理的时间间隔和安排的顺序，一般而言爆发力训练需要安排在训练课的前半部分，这时运动员的体力和精力充沛，训练效果会更好。在进行爆发力训练时也应注意要让机体在充分恢复的情况下再进行下一组练习，否则机体代谢的方式就不是无氧代谢，更多的是糖酵解供能或有氧氧化供能，达不到爆发力训练的目的。

The plyometric training method is an effective training method commonly used in current athletes' explosive power training. In the process of application, this method can effectively improve the strength and sensitivity of athletes' lower limb neuromuscular system, and has a very effective effect on improving athletes' lower limb explosive power. Plyometric muscle strength training means to fast dynamic load pull of muscles, and to produce the explosive muscle contraction in the process. In the process of training, the teacher will let the student through a series of movements, to make muscles fast to the centrifugal contraction, then into the centripetal contraction, and so repeat cyclically to keep the lower limb muscle contraction. This kind of plyometric training is mainly based on various jumping exercises. In this process, students can not only improve the explosive power of muscles, but also effectively enhance the coordination of take-off movements and increase the reaction speed and strength of lower limb muscles. When using plyometric training, we should pay attention to the reasonable time interval and the order of arrangement. Generally speaking, explosive force training should be arranged in the first half of the training class. At this time, the athletes' physical strength and energy are abundant, and so the training effect will be better. During the explosive force training, attention should also be paid to make the body perform the next set of exercises under the condition of full recovery. Otherwise, the metabolic mode of the body will not have anaerobic metabolism, but glycolysis function or aerobic oxidation energy supply, which cannot achieve the purpose of explosive force training.

2 大幅度训练法
2 Large scale training method

大幅度训练法指的是让学生在进行爆发力训练的过程中，增强学生动作的幅度，使学生在运动时，充分对肢体的各个关节和肌肉进行练习，在增加动作幅度的过程中，增强肌肉力量，以此来提高肌肉爆发力。这种大幅度训练法，在应用的过程中，需要考虑到增加技术动作的加速距离，提高技术动作的力量，所以在练习的过程中，不仅能够增强运动员的肌肉力量，还能够有效提高其身体各部位的柔韧性，对于运动员的整体身体素质提高也十分有利。这种大幅度训练法在应用的过程中，主要以举重等练习为主，这种大幅度的练习过程中，学生的肌肉会进行充分的收缩，以此来激发学生的肌肉力量，使肌肉在等长的静力性收缩状态下不断提升力量，从而增强肌肉的最大力量，增强肌肉爆发力。在进行大幅度力量训练时要注意实施区别对待原则，不同学生身体素质尤其是柔韧素质不同，稍有不慎可能造成肌肉拉伤，应该在运动员充分活动身体的基础上逐渐提高动作的幅度，也应遵循循序渐进的原则，将柔韧练习和力量练习结合起来，相互促进，不可有偏颇。

The lavge-scale training method refers to enhancing the range of students' movements in the process of explosive force training, so that the students can fully exercise each joint and muscle of the limbs during the exercise, and enhance the muscle strength in the process of increasing the range of movements, so as to improve the explosive force of muscles. This training method, in the process of application, you need to consider to increase the acceleration of technical movement distance, improve the power of the technique, so in the process of practice, not only can enhance the muscle strength of athletes, but also can effectively improve the flexibility of all parts of the body, and it is also very good for athletes to improve the quality of the whole body. This training method in the process of application, is used mainly in weightlifting exercises. It is a dramatic practice process, the muscles of the students will be fully contracted, so as to inspire students muscle strength, to make the muscle in long static contraction condition for improved strength, and thereby to create the greatest power of muscles, and enhance the muscle power. In big strength training, we should pay attention to the implementation of the principle of distinction between different students' physical quality, especially the flexible quality, which may be affected by any carelessness and will cause muscle strain. It should be on the basis of full activity of athlet's, body gradually to improve the range of motion in exercises, and also should follow the principle of gradual ness, combine flexibility exercise and strength training, in order to promote each other, and there shall be no bias.

3　递增训练法
3　Incremental training method

递增训练法是当前比较常用的一种爆发力训练方法之一，在应用的过程中，主要是通过逐渐增加阻力的方法,使得学生负荷的重量和动作速度能够得到稳步提高,让学生在掌握基础的训练标准之后,逐渐增加训练量,以此来达到动作和速度的极限。在该过程中,学生的肌肉力量和爆发力就会得到稳步提高,而且能够有效提高学生的速度。这种递增训练法属于一种极有规划的长期训练方法,在训练的过程中,教师需要将整个训练过程划分为几个阶段,然后对每个阶段的训练内容进行合理规划,保证其中的力量、速度和爆发力训练的强度能够适合学生,使学生的爆发力得到稳步提高,避免因使用不当或急于求成而造成不必要的运动损伤。递增负荷训练法并不是一直增加负荷,而是在合理的范围内,根据运动员的差异设定不同的范围,同时要注意在进行递增负荷训练时要兼顾负荷量和练习速度,同时要注意力量训练与专项速度的转化,提高转化率才有利于专项成绩的提高。

The incremental training method is currently one of the more commonly used a explosive force training method, in the process of application, mainly by the method of increasing resistance makes student load weight and movement speed to be improved steadily, lets the student after mastering the basic training standards, gradually increase the volume of training, in order to achieve action and speed limit. In the process, students' muscle strength and explosive force can be improved steadily, and also it can effectively improve the speed of students. Incremental training method is a method of planning of long-term training in the training process.The whole process of training, needs to be divided into several stages, and then it is necessary to make a reasonable plann for each phase of the training content, in order to ensure the strength, speed, and the intensity of explosive force training can be suitable for high school students, and make the explosive force of high school students will be increased steadily, and avoid unnecessary injuries caused by improper use or rush sports. Incremental load training method may not always to increase the load, but if needs to set different range within a reasonable range, according to different athletes, and at the same time it should pay attention to when the increasing load training should be balancd with load and speed, and pay attention to the special strength training and speed of transformation. Improving the conversion rate is beneficial to the improvement of the specific performance.

一般而言递增负荷训练法在学生准备期和比赛期的前期使用频率较高,有利于使机体产生力逐步提升。同时我们也要积极吸收和借鉴先进的训练理念和方法，例如爆发力量训练、身体功能训练和运动表现训练等，将其应用到我们的日常训练中，尤其是针对高水平的学生而言，辅之专项性较高的训练方法手段效果会更好。

Generally speaking, the method of incremental load training is frequently used in the preparation period for competition and the early stage of the competition period, which is conducive to the gradual improvement of the body's production force. At the same time, we should actively absorb and learn from advanced training concepts and methods, such as exclosive power training, physical function training, sports performance training and apply them to our daily training. If supplemented by special training methods and means especially for high-level students. It will have better effects.

第二节　徒手爆发力训练方法
Section 2　Unarmed explosive force training method

1　上肢爆发力徒手训练方法
1　Freehand training method for explosive power of upper limbs

1.1　爆发式俯卧撑
1.1　Explosive push-ups

锻炼部位

Exercise site

上肢，包括胸部肌群和肱三头肌。

The upper limbs, including the pectoral muscles and the triceps.

图3-2-1　爆发式俯卧撑

动作要领

Essentials of Action

① 俯卧于地面的薄垫上，做俯卧撑姿势。

① Lie prone on a thin mat on the ground and do push-ups.

② 快速上推身体使身体悬空，将整个手臂垂直作用于地面，双臂完全伸展，通过固定核心肌群保持身体竖直。

② Quickly push the body up to make the body suspended, apply the whole body weight vertically to the ground, fully extend the arms, and keep the body upright by fixing the core muscle groups.

③ 由于重力作用,控制身体,回到地面上(注:如果训练者无法保持标准的俯卧撑姿势,可以先训练上肢力量和核心稳定性,再进行该项练习)。

③ Due to the effect of gravity, control the body and return to the ground (Note: If the trainer is unable to maintain the standard push-up position, upper body strength and core stability can be trained before doing this exercise).

负荷强度

Load strength

一组15次,做3组,组间休息15秒。

Do 3 sets of 15 reps with a 15-second break between sets.

注意事项

Notes

① 保持姿势的稳定性。

① Maintain the stability of the posture.

② 动作要有爆发性。

② The action should be explosive.

③ 由于该训练爆发力较强,腕部或肩部受伤的训练者不要进行训练。

③ Due to the strong explosive force of this training, the trainers with wrist or shoulder injuries should not do the training.

1.2 击掌俯卧撑

1.2 High-five push-ups

锻炼部位

Exercise site

上肢,包括胸部肌群和肱三头肌。

The upper limbs, including the pectoral muscles and the triceps.

图3-2-2　击掌俯卧撑

动作要领

Essentials of action

① 双手扶地与肩同宽，手关节伸直双手手掌外翻，手指指向大约45°角的位置。

① Hold the ground with your hands shoulder-width apart, keep the joints straight and turn the palms of your hands outward with your fingers pointing to an angle of about 45 degrees.

② 身体下压，肘关节始终保持在腕关节的正上方，且与躯干呈45°角。

② Keep the elbow joint directly above the wrist and at a 45 degrees angle with the trunk.

③ 肘关节小于90°时，身体迅速向上移动，同时双手抬离地面快速击掌一次。

③ When the elbow joint is less than 90 degrees, move your body up quickly and lift your hands off the ground for a quick high-five.

④ 然后重新返回地面，着地时的动作要尽可能轻柔缓慢，同时为下一次重复运动做好准备。

④ Then return to the ground, landing as gently and slowly as possible, and prepare for the next repetition.

负荷强度

Load strength

每组5~7个，做3组，组间休息15秒（初学者次数不宜过多）。

Do 3 sets of 5 to 7, with a 15-second break between sets (Not too many times for beginners).

注意事项

Notes

① 在俯卧撑动作的最低点时，手臂与躯干呈45°角。

① At the lowest point of push-ups, the arms should be at a 45 degrees angle to the torso.

② 在身体其他部位向上抬之前，臀部与上一运动过程中身体始终成一条直线。

② Before the rest of the body is lifted up, the hips remain in line with the body during the previous movement.

2　下肢爆发力徒手训练方法
2　Freehand training method for lower limb explosive power

2.1　垂直向上跳
2.1　Jump straight up

锻炼部位

Exercise site

小腿三头肌（腓肠肌与比目鱼肌）。

Triceps of the lower leg (gastrocnemius and soleus).

动作要领

Essentials of action

① 蓄势准备：双脚和肩等宽或略宽于肩呈站立姿态。接着向躯干两侧快速摆动双臂，同时弯曲大腿，臀部后坐，为腿部加满能量。

① Ready: Standing with feet equal to or slightly wider than shoulders. Then quickly swing your arms to both side of the torso, while bending your thighs and hips to sit back while bending your hips and knees to refuel your legs.

② 爆发：快速向上挥动双臂，延伸臀部与膝盖，接着拔地而起。往上跳起时充分伸展踝、膝、髋三关节。

② Explosion: Quickly wave your arms up, extend your hips and knees, and then rise to your feet. Landing with ankle, knee, and hip joints fully extended when jumping up.

图 3-2-3　垂直向上跳

负荷强度

Load strength

一组10次，做3组，组间休息15秒。

Do 3 sets of 10 with a 15 seconds break between sets.

注意事项

Notes

① 脚尖着地过渡到脚跟吸收冲力，同时屈髋屈膝深蹲姿势准备缓冲。

① Transition from tiptoe to heel to absorb impact, with hip and knee flexes as a cushion.

② 膝盖与脚尖为一条直线，膝盖千万别内倾。

② Knees and toes are in a straight line, knees do not lean inwards.

2.2 开合跳

2.2 Jumping jacks

锻炼部位

Exercise site

股二头肌与小腿三头肌（腓肠肌与比目鱼肌）。

Biceps femoris and triceps of the lower leg (gastrocnemius and soleus).

图3-2-4 开合跳

动作要领

Essentials of action

① 呈自然站立姿态，双腿向外跳开，膝关节自然弯曲，髋关节自然向外展开。

① Stand in a natural posture, with legs jumping outward, knees bending naturally and hips unrolling naturally.

② 两腿分开距离大于肩宽，膝盖、脚尖向外。

② The distance between legs is greater than the shoulder width, knees and toes pointing out.

③ 向内跳回：双脚/足跟并拢，脚尖向前或外开。

③ Jump back in: Feet close together, toes forward or out.

④ 上体以脊柱为中轴线，保持自然直立。

④ The upper body takes the spine as the central axis and maintains a natural upright position.

负荷强度

Load strength

一组做25次，共做3组，组间休息15秒。

Do 3 sets of 25 reps with a 15 seconds break between sets.

注意事项

Notes

① 体重严重超标的人不能盲目开合跳。

① People who are seriously overweight should not jump blindly.

② 膝盖受伤的人不建议做。

② It is not recommended for people with knee injuries.

③ 跳的过程中要保持对身体的控制。

③ Keep your body in control during the jump.

2.3 跳台阶

2.3 The dance steps

锻炼部位

Exercise site

股四头肌（股直肌、股内侧肌、股外侧肌与股中间肌）、缝匠肌与小腿三头肌（腓肠肌与比目鱼肌）。

Quadriceps femoris (rectus femoris, vastus medialis, vastus lateralis and vastus intermedius), sartorius and calf triceps (gastrocnemius and soleus).

图3-2-5 跳台阶

动作要领

Essentials of action

① 训练者站在楼梯或台阶前。

① The trainer stands in front of the stairs or steps.

② 双臂自然前后摆动，同时双脚猛蹬地面呈立定跳远状，连续跳上2、3、4层楼梯或台阶，然后循环往复。

② Swing your arms back and forth naturally, and at the same time push your feet off the ground in the form of a standing long jump. Jump up 2, 3 or 4 floors of stairs or steps continuously, and then repeat.

负荷强度

Load strength

一组跳10~15个台阶，做3~5组，组间休息30秒。

Jump 10-15 steps in one group, do 3-5 sets, rest for 30 seconds between groups.

注意事项

Notes

① 跳台阶的过程中需要上肢肌肉、腰腹肌肉和下肢肌肉相互配合发力，既为了起跳，又保障平衡。

① The process of jumping steps requires upper limb muscles, lumbar and abdominal muscles and lower limb muscles to cooperate with each other to generate strength, not only for taking off, but also to ensure balance.

② 跳台阶的时候要注意选择一些不是很陡同时台面很宽的楼梯或台阶，防止出现危险。

② When jumping the steps, pay attention to choose some stairs or steps that are not too steep and have a wide mesa to avoid danger.

2.4 原地纵跳摸高

2.4 Touch height by jumping in place

锻炼部位

Exercise site

小腿三头肌（腓肠肌与比目鱼肌）、腓骨长肌和腓骨短肌。

Calf triceps (gastrocnemius and soleus), fibula longus and fibula brevis.

动作要领

Essentials of Action

① 原地纵跳：训练者站在地面上，双臂迅速前后摆动后双脚猛蹬离开地面。

① In-situ vertical jump: the trainer stands on the ground, quickly swinging his arms back and forth and kicking his feet off the ground.

② 摸高：手臂伸直朝向跳起的方向进行摸高。

② Touch height: touch height with arms straight toward the direction of jumping.

图 3-2-6 原地纵跳摸高

负荷强度

Load strength

一组做5~8次，做3~5组，组间休息15秒。

Do 5-8 reps for 3-5 reps, with a 15 seconds break between sets.

注意事项

Attention

① 两脚左右开立，与肩同宽，两臂前后摆动，前摆时，两腿伸直，后摆时，屈膝降低重心，上体稍前倾，手臂尽量往后摆。

① Open your feet from side to side, shoulder-width apart. Swing your arms back and forth. When swinging forward, straighten your legs. When swinging back, bend your knees and lower your weight.

② 上下肢动作协调配合，摆动时一伸二屈降重心，上体稍前倾。

② Coordinate upper and lower limb movements. When swinging, one extends and two bends to lower the center of gravity, and the upper body slightly leans forward.

③ 原地纵跳+摸高的方式锻炼训练者的下肢快速爆发能力，培养训练者的快速起跳能力。

③ The way of vertical jump in situ + touch height exercises the trainers' ability to break out quickly in lower limbs, and cultivates the trainers' ability to jump quickly.

2.5　侧向跳跃

2.5　Side jump

锻炼部位

Exercise site

小腿三头肌（腓肠肌与比目鱼肌）和股二头肌。

Calf triceps (gastrocnemius and soleus) and biceps femoris.

动作要领

Essentials of Action

①右腿单脚站立，左腿通过膝盖弯曲从地面抬起。

① Stand on one leg and lift the left leg from the ground through knee bending.

②右腿微屈身体下蹲，身体朝左侧开始做动作，以45°角用力向远处跳。

② The right leg slightly bends the body to squat down, the body starts to do the movement to the left, with 45 degrees of strength to the distance jump.

③以左脚单腿下蹲姿势轻轻落地。屈膝重新朝身体右侧跳跃，重复以上动作。

③ Squat gently on the ground with one leg left. Return to the right side of your body and repeat.

图3-2-7 侧向跳跃

负荷强度

Load strength

一组8~12个,做4~6组,组间休息15秒。

Do 4-6 sets of 8-12, with a 15 seconds break between sets.

注意事项

Notes

① 落地时膝关节放松成蹲踞姿势,确保身体能够获得最大的缓冲力,并为下一次跳跃积蓄最大的力量。

① Relax your knees into a squatting position when you hit the ground to ensure that your body can get the maximum cushion and build up the maximum force for the next jump.

② 双脚每次着地时，膝盖应与脚趾保持在一条直线上；无论什么时候，两侧膝盖都不能内扣。

② Keep knees and toes in a straight line each time the feet land; neither knee should be buckled inside at any time.

③ 膝盖受伤的人不建议做。

③ Tis not recommended for people with knee injuries.

④ 身体朝45°角方向跳起，每次运动都应竭尽全力。

④ Jump with your body at a 45 degrees Angle. Try your best every time you move.

2.6 波比跳

2.6 Burpee

锻炼部位

Exercise site

股四头肌（股直肌、股内侧肌、股外侧肌和股中间肌）、股二头肌、小腿三头肌（腓肠肌与比目鱼肌）、肱三头肌和部分胸部肌群。

Quadriceps femoris (rectus femoris, vastus medialis, vastus lateralis and vastus intermedius), biceps femoris, calf triceps (gastrocnemius and soleus), triceps of the humerus and part of the pectoralis muscle group.

动作要领

Essentials of Action

① 开始时呈站立姿势。

① Stand at the beginning.

② 将大腿后侧肌群往后推，尽可能地保持小腿垂直，双膝呈中立姿势，髋关节转轴往前弯，手掌接触地面，手指朝前。保持下背平直，双脚在双手碰地时往后伸或滑到后方。

② Push back the muscles at the back of the thighs, keep the calves perpendicular as far as possible, keep the knees neutral, bend the axis of rotation of the hip joint forward, place the palm on the ground and point your fingers forward.

Keep your lower back straight and extend or slide your feet back when your hands touch the ground.

③ 双脚往后滑,摆出伏地挺身最高位置的姿势。

③ Slide your feet back into a pushup position.

图 3-2-8 波比跳

④ 胸部往地面沉的同时，手肘紧贴躯干两侧，肩膀与手腕上下对齐。

④ As your chest sinks toward the floor, elbows close to the sides of the torso and line your shoulders with your wrists up and down.

⑤ 用爆发式动作伸展手肘，髋部往上推到完全伸展，膝盖往胸部位置贴近。

⑤ Stretch your elbows in an explosive motion, push your hips up to full stretch, and pull your knees toward your chest.

⑥ 双腿拉到身体下方时，试着用双脚取代双手的位置。尽可能保持双脚平直，打直背部，抵达深蹲的最低位置。

⑥ As you pull your legs under your body, try replacing your hands with your feet. Keep your feet as straight as possible and straighten your back to the lowest squat position.

⑦ 身体推离深蹲最低位置，垂直往上跳。

⑦ Push the body away from the lowest position of squat and jump up vertically.

负荷强度

Load strength

一组8次，共做4组，组间休息20秒。

Do 4 sets of 8 reps with a 20 seconds break between sets.

注意事项

Notes

①波比跳前应该先做热身活动3-5分钟，热身完之后，要注意不能立刻开始，先做俯卧撑和深蹲动作，使身体进入运动状态。

① Burpee should first do warm-up exercises for 3-5 minutes, after finishing, pay attention not to start immediately, do push-ups and squats first to get your body into motion.

②如果运动中有疼痛感、头晕或任何身体不适，请立即停止。这表示你的身体状况不适宜如此高强度的训练。

② If you feel pain, dizziness or any physical discomfort during the exercise, stop immediately. This means your body is not fit for such intense training.

③ 有高血压、糖尿病、心脏病或者心血管疾病等，在运动前应当咨询医生。

③ If you have hypertension, diabetes, heart disease or cardiovascular disease, you should consult your doctor before exercising.

④ 女性在做波比跳时，伏地挺身可以用膝盖跪地方式来进行，或者省略掉也可以。

④ For women, pushups can be performed on the knees or omitted when doing burpees.

2.7 蛙跳
2.7 Leapfrog

锻炼部位

Exercise site

股四头肌（股直肌、股内侧肌、股外侧肌与股中间肌）、缝匠肌和股二头肌。

Quadriceps femoris (rectus femoris, vastus medialis, vastus lateralis and vastus intermedius), sartorius and biceps femoris.

动作要领

Essentials of Action

① 双手置于头后站立。

① Stand with hands behind head.

② 深蹲，保持躯干直立，头部朝向正前方，眼睛平视。

② Squat, keeping torso upright with head facing straight forward, eyes straight ahead.

③ 向前跳几十公分，避免跳起不必要的高度。

③ Jump dozens of centimeters forward to avoid jumping unnecessary height.

④ 当双脚接触地面时，用双腿缓冲落地的影响，然后再次跳起。

④ When your feet touch the ground, use your legs to cushion the impact of landing, and then jump again.

图3-2-9 蛙跳

负荷强度

Load strength

一组10次,一次3组,组间休息30秒。

Do 3 sets of 10 reps with a 30 seconds break between sets.

注意事项

Notes

① 训练强度需要循序渐进,根据个人情况进行调整。

① Training intensity should be adjusted step by step according to personal conditions.

② 在空中要把腹肌充分拉开,也就是展腹。

② In the air to fully open the abdominal muscles, also known as abdominal spread.

③ 动作连贯,要注意缓冲,脚落地的时候应该是脚后跟先着地,再是脚尖着地。

③ Coherent movement, pay attention to cushion, when the heel landing should be tiptoe first, then foot landing.

2.8 弓步交叉跳
2.8 Cross lunges

锻炼部位

Exercise site

股四头肌（股直肌、股内侧肌、股外侧肌与股中间肌）、缝匠肌、半腱肌、半膜肌和小腿三头肌（腓肠肌与比目鱼肌）。

Quadriceps femoris (rectus femoris, vastus medialis, vastus lateralis and vastus intermedius), sartorius, semitendinosus, semimembranous and calf triceps (gastrocnemius and soleus).

图3-2-10　弓步交叉跳

动作要领

Essentials of Action

① 双脚前后站立，后脚脚后跟抬离地面，将全身重心压在前腿。

① Stand with your feet back and forth, lifting your heels off the ground and placing the center of your body on your front legs.

② 髋关节折叠使躯干前倾，前腿微屈。

② The hip joint is folded so that the trunk leans forward and the forelegs are slightly bent.

③ 身体用力向上跳的同时前后脚交叉，前脚置于后方，后脚置于前方，双脚着地时恢复开始姿势，只是前后腿互换位置。再次向上跳起并重复以上动作。

③ Jump with your front and rear feet crossed, with your front feet in the rear and your back feet in the front. When you land on your feet, you will resume your posture, but the front and rear legs will switch positions. Jump up again and repeat.

负荷强度

Load strength

一组左右腿各8~12次，做3~5组，组间休息15秒。

Do 3 to 5 sets of 8 to 12 times of left and right legs, with a 15 seconds break between sets.

注意事项

Notes

① 着地的动作要尽量放轻，每一次着地时，都要为下一次跳跃做好准备。

① Landing should be as light as possible, and each time you land, you should be ready for the next jump.

② 双脚每次着地时，膝盖应与脚趾保持在一条直线上，双腿膝盖绝不能朝身体中间位置并拢。

② When your feet land each time, your knees should be in line with your toes, and your knees should never come together toward the middle of your body.

③ 双脚每次着地时髋关节弯曲，同时脊柱挺直。

③ Bend your hips and straighten your spine each time your feet touch the ground.

④ 每次身体向上跳起时，躯干尽量上抬。

④ Every time the body up to jump up, the torso as much as possible.

2.9 单腿跳跃
2.9 Jump on one leg

锻炼部位

Exercise site

小腿三头肌（腓肠肌与比目鱼肌）、胫骨前肌与腓骨长肌和腓骨短肌。

Calf triceps （gastrocnemius and soleus）, tibia anterior and fibula longus and fibula brevis.

图3-2-11　单腿跳跃

动作要领

Essentials of Action

① 在身前排列一排适当高度障碍物。

① Arrange a row of obstacles of appropriate height in front of you.

② 单腿站立保持平衡。

② Stand on one leg to keep balance.

③ 向前跳越过障碍物，跳起、越过和落地使用同一条腿。

③ Jump forward over obstacles, using the same leg for jumping, crossing and landing.

④ 用相同的方式跳跃障碍物，到达尽头后，转身，用另一条腿跳回起点。

④ Jump the obstacle in the same way. After reaching the end, turn around and jump back to the starting point with the other leg.

负荷强度

Load strength

一组10~15次，做3~5组，组间休息15秒。

Do 3 to 5 sets of 10 to 15 time with a 15 seconds break between sets.

注意事项

Notes

① 过程中需要上肢肌肉、腰腹肌肉和下肢肌肉相互配合发力。

① The process requires the coordination of upper limb muscles, lumbar and abdominal muscles and lower limb muscles.

② 膝盖受伤的人不建议做。

② It is not recommended for people with knee injuries.

③ 上下肢动作协调配合，摆动时一伸二屈降重心，上体稍前倾。

③ Coordination of upper and lower limb movements, one extension and two bending to lower the center of gravity when swinging, the upper body slightly forward.

④ 障碍物高度不宜过高，根据个人情况选择调整。

④ The height of the obstacle should not be too high. It should be adjusted according to personal circumstances.

第四章　爆发力训练——单一器械

Chapter 4　Explosive power training—single apparatus

第一节　杠铃训练方法

Section 1　Barbell training methods

1　杠铃上肢练习

1　Barbell upper limb exercise

1.1　杠铃仰卧推举

1.1　Barbell bench press

主要锻炼肌肉

The main exercise muscles

三角肌前束、三角肌中束、胸大肌、胸小肌和肱三头肌。

Anterior deltoid, middle deltoid, pectoralis major, pectoralis minor and triceps brachii.

动作要领

Action tips

① 躺在水平放置的健身椅上，双脚平放在地面上头部始终放在健身椅上。

① Lie on the horizontal fitness chair, keep your feet on the ground and head on the chair.

第四章　爆发力训练——单一器械

② 双手抓住杠铃的横杆，掌心向上，双手伸展宽度超过肩膀。

② Hold the bar of the barbell with both hands, palms up, and make your hands wider than your shoulders.

③ 将杠铃从架子上取下，抓住横杆，双臂伸直与肩关节保持垂直。

③ Remove the barbell from the rack and grasp the bar, keeping your arms straight and perpendicular to your shoulder joints.

④ 将横杆下降到胸部，中央肘部与横杆始终成一条直线，并位于横杆下面。

④ Lower the bar to the chest, with the central elbows always in a straight line with the bar, and keep the elbows under the crossbar.

⑤ 当横杆位于最低点时，将其推回到起始位置。

⑤ When the bar is at its lowest point, push it back to the starting position.

图4-1-1　杠铃仰卧推举

负荷强度

Intensity

① 快速卧推3~5组，每组重量为最大重量的40%，每组5~8个。

① 3-5 sets of rapid bench presses, 40% of max weight per set, 5~8 per set.

② 卧推3-6组，每组重量为最大重量的80%~90%，每组8~12个。

② Bench presses 3-6 sets, 80%-90% of maximum weight per sets, 8-12 per set.

注意事项

Attentions

① 无论做任何训练动作，最初时跟杠铃、哑铃或其他用具的接触是十分重要的，在准备卧推时，先躺在健身椅上，请确保你的臀部、腰部、上背及头部都稳稳地放在健身椅上，双眼要跟杠铃成一直线。

① Initial contact with a barbell, dumbbell, or other equipments is very important in any training exercise. When preparing for the bench press, lie on the fitness chair first. Make sure your hips, waist, upper back and head are firmly placed on the chair, and your eyes should be in line with the barbell.

② 双脚可以放在不同的位置，因为每个人的习惯及生理结构都有所不同，但前提是请确保双脚可以透过地面稳稳地发力，不妨试试不同的位置。

② As everyone's habits and physiology are different, you can place your feet in different positions, but make sure that your feet can work steadily through the floor, so don't be afraid to try different positions.

③ 无论是窄手、阔手或是一般的握法，都能训练胸部，不过由于每个人的生理结构有些许不同，大家可以试试哪种握法最适合你发力。同时，握铃距离也不宜一成不变，中间做出微调，能有效地刺激肌肉。

③ Whether it is a narrow hand, wide hand or normal grip, it is possible to train the chest, but since everyone's physiological structure is slightly different, you can try to find out which grip is most suitable for you to exert force. Also the grip distance should not be unchanged, you can adjust the distance slightly to stimulate the muscles effectively.

④ 收紧全身肌肉；从技巧层面来说，收紧全身肌肉是一个完美卧推的基础。

④ Tightening the muscles of the whole body; technically, tightening the muscles of the whole body is the foundation of a perfect bench press.

1.2 斜角杠铃推举
1.2 Oblique barbell push

主要锻炼肌肉
The main exercise muscles
三角肌。
Deltoid.

动作要领
Action tips

双脚分开站立与肩同宽，将杠铃的一端放在墙角处或固定装置中，单手握住另一端。用力将杠铃向上推举，使其与手掌保持几厘米的间距，然后另一只手抓住它，把它放回到你的肩部，再次将杠铃用力向上推，使其保持在手掌前方几厘米的距离，另一只手抓住，慢慢地将它放回到最开始的一侧肩膀上，这样就完成了一次完整的重复动作。

Stand with your feet apart as shoulder-width and place one end of the barbell in a corner or in a fixture, holding the other end in one hand. Push the barbell up hard enough to make it away from your palm, then grab it with your other hand and lower it back to your

图4-1-2　斜角杠铃推举

75

shoulder, push the barbell up hard enough again by this hand and grab it with your first hand, then slowly lower it back to your shoulder on the side you started with, by that, you have completed it once.

① 每次用手抓杠铃时，双膝和双臂同时弯曲来缓冲下落的冲击力。

① Each time you grab the barbell with your one hand, bend both knees and arms at the same time to cushion the impact of the fall.

② 每次抓住或抛出杠铃时，躯体可以有小幅度的转动。

② Your body can rotate slightly each time the barbell is caught or thrown.

负荷强度

Intensity

选择适宜的重量，在做功速度不减慢的情况下每组8-10次，做4组，每组间歇1分钟。

Choose your appropriate weight, do 4 sets of 8-10 reps per set without slowing down the rate, with a 1 minute break between sets.

注意事项

Attentions

① 控制杠铃是最重要的元素。为了产生大量的功率，必须能够处理更大量的作功，在接杠时维持一个好的基底，同时爆发式地将杠铃推起。换手接杠铃时注意要顺着杠铃下落的轨迹做一个缓冲，并顺势向上。

① Controlling the barbell is most important. In order to creat a lot of power, you must be able to handle a larger rate of work, maintain a good base while catching the bar, and push the barbell up explosively. When switching hands to catch the barbell, be sure to cushion the barbell follow the downward trajectory and then make it upward.

② 爆发力训练过程中，重量不宜过大，向上推举速度越快越好。

② During explosive strength training, the weights should not be too heavy and the faster the upward thrust, the better the effect.

2 杠铃腿部练习
2 Barbell leg exercise

2.1 杠铃颈后深蹲
2.1 Back of the neck barbell squat

主要锻炼肌肉

The main exercise muscles

股二头肌、股四头肌、臀大肌、臀中肌和臀小肌。

Biceps femoris, quadriceps femoris, gluteus maximus, gluteus medius and gluteus minimus.

图4-1-3 杠铃颈后深蹲

动作要领

Action tips

将杠铃横放于肩上，不要放在颈部，双脚分开站立，比肩略宽，脚趾向外翻转10~15°。过程：膝关节和髋关节同时弯曲，整个身体朝地面下压，尽可能地压低，但下背部依然保持拱起姿势，等到身体无法继续下压时做反向动作，重新站起来。

Put the barbell across your shoulders, not on your neck, and stand with your feet slightly wider than shoulder-width apart, turning your toes outward 10-15 degrees. Process: bend your knees and hips at the same time and press your entire body down towards the ground as low as you can, while still keep your lower back in an arched position, then do the reverse when your body can no longer continue to press and stand back up.

负荷强度

Intensity

4～6组，每组8～12个，重量建议从最轻依次递增。

4-6 sets, 8-12 per sets, weight recommendations in ascending order from lightest.

注意事项

Attentions

① 重量不宜过大，站起时要脚趾发力，做提踵动作，脚后跟离开地面。

① The weight should not be too heavy, make the toes work and do a heel lift with your heels off the groundwhen you stand up.

② 双腿膝关节不能朝身体中线内扣，膝盖与脚趾应保持在同一条直线上。

② The knees of both legs should not buckle in toward the midline of your body, and the knees and toes should be in the same line.

③ 需要稍微调整一下双脚间的距离，找到一个最适合自己的站位。

③ You need to adjust the distance between your feet slightly to find a distance that works best for you.

④ 重量适中，蹲下速度应是缓慢的，站起速度则越快越好。

④ Keep the weight moderate, the squat should be slow and the faster you stand up the better.

2.2 杠铃下蹲提踵
2.2 Barbell squats and heel lift

主要锻炼肌肉

The main exercise muscles

腓肠肌和比目鱼肌。

Genito skin and ratio fish skin.

图4-1-4　杠铃下蹲提踵

动作要领

Action tips

这项运动与杠铃颈后深蹲的运动机制一致，唯一不同之处在于动作最高点时的结束动作将杠铃横放于肩上，不要放在颈部，双脚分开站立，比肩略宽，脚趾向外翻转 10~15°。膝关节和髋关节同时弯曲，整个身体朝地面下压，尽可能地压低，但下背部依然保持拱起姿势，等到身体已经无法继续压低时做反向动作，重新站起来，在每次动作的最高点时，通过脚趾用力下踩，脚后跟用力上抬的方式完成提踵动作，前脚掌着地，然后脚后跟触地，使身体慢慢落下并恢复下蹲姿势完成整套动作。

This exercise has the same mechanics as the barbell back squat, with the only difference being that the barbell is placed across the shoulders instead of the neck at the end of the movement at its highest point, and the feet stand slightly wider than shoulder-width apart, with the toes turned outward 10 to 15 degrees.Bend your knees and hips at the same time and lower your entire body toward the ground as far down as possible, but still keep your lower back in an arched position, and when you can no longer lower your body any further, do the reverse and stand back up.At the top of each movement, step on your toes and lift your heels up to complete the heel lift, landing on your front feet, then drop your heels to the ground, slowly lowering your body and returning to a squat position to complete the set.

① 身体下落，恢复下蹲姿势时，脚后跟不能抬离地面，只有当身体站直，并且在动作最高点时，脚后跟才能从地面抬起。

① When the body returns to the squatting position, the heels cannot be lifted off the ground, and can only be lifted from the ground when the body is standing straight and at the highest point of the movement.

② 一口气流畅地完成整套上下起伏的动作。

② Perform the entire set of up and down movements smoothly in one go.

③ 双腿膝关节不能朝身体中线内扣，膝盖与脚趾应保持在同一条直线上。

③ The knees of both legs should not buckle inward, and the knees and toes should be kept in the same straight line.

④ 你可能需要稍微调整一下脚尖的距离，找到一个适合自己的站位。

④ You may need to adjust the distance between your toes slightly to find a stance that suits you.

负荷强度:

Intensity:

4~6组,每组8~12个,重量建议从最轻依次递增。

4-6 sets, 8-12 per set, we recommend increasing the weight from the lightest to the highest.

注意事项

Attentions

① 注意完成动作时不要屈膝、屈体;控制重心不要有意前移,否则效果极差,可在前脚掌下垫一块铃片防止重心前移。

① Don't bend your knees and body when completing the movement; don't intentionally move your center of gravity forward when controlling it, otherwise the effect will be extremely poor, a bell piece can be placed under the forefoot to prevent the center of gravity from shifting forward.

② 各种提踵动作因站法不同,所锻炼的部位也有所差异。脚尖向内扣站法侧重于锻炼腓肠肌的内侧头,而普通站法内外侧都能练到。

② Because of the different stances, the parts that are exercised by the heel lift also differ. The stance with the toes buckled inwards focuses on exercising the inner side of the gastrocnemius muscle, while the ordinary stance can exercise the inner and outer sides.

③ 提踵动作主要是以腓肠肌的收缩来完成的。提起脚跟时,感到小腿肌群的充分收缩,稍停顿后再缓慢下落至最低限度,使小腿肌得到充分伸展。

③ The heel lift relies mainly on the systolic of the gastrocnemius muscle. When lifting the heel, you should feel the full systolic of the calf muscle group, pause briefly and then slowly drop down to the minimum to allow the calf muscle to be fully extended.

④ 小腿练习时的感觉是非常明显的,不要被开始时的酸胀感觉所迷惑。锻炼小腿的重点要放在重复次数上,要多坚持直到力竭为止才会产生锻炼的效果;另外,动作一定要标准,对小腿的刺激才会更加明显。

④ The sensation in the calves during the exercise is very pronounced, don't be confused by the soreness at the beginning of the exercise. The key to exercising the calves is to focus on the number of repetitions, and to keep going more until you can't get up do that; in addition, the more standard the movement, the more obvious the calf stimulation will be.

2.3 单腿罗马尼亚硬拉
2.3 One leg romania style dead lift

主要锻炼肌肉

The main exercise muscles

臀大肌、臀中肌、臀小肌和股二头肌。

Gluteus maximus、gluteus medius、gluteus minimus and biceps femoris.

图4-1-5 单腿罗马尼亚硬拉

动作要领
Action tips

身体呈直立姿态单腿站位，右腿稍离地面，右手紧握自制重物，重量适当，手臂伸直，将重物自然放在身体前方，左手置于体侧，左腿屈膝半蹲，右腿伸直后抬起至几乎与身体呈一条直线，以支撑腿的髋部肌群发力拉直身体。

The body is in an upright posture standing on one leg, the right leg slightly off the ground, straighten your arm, grasp a homemade weight with your right hand and place it in front of your body, put your left hand on your side, squat with your left leg, straighten your right leg and raise it so that your body is almost parallel to the ground, use the hip muscle group of the supporting leg to straighten your body.

负荷强度
Intensity

8~10 次/组，3~4 组，每组间歇时间 1 分钟。

8-10 times per set, 3-4 sets, 1 minute rest time between each set.

注意事项
Attentions

① 注意保持背部伸直，腹部收紧，控制好身体重心和姿态。

① Be sure to keep your back straight, tighten your belly, and control your center of gravity and posture.

② 头、背部和腿全程尽量保持同一水平线。

② Try to keep your head, back and legs always at the same level.

③ 髋关节角度至关重要，保持躯干始终与地面平行，不要左右乱晃。

③ The angle of the hip joint is crucial, keep your torso parallel to the ground and don't sway.

第二节 壶铃训练方法
Section 2　Kettlebell training methods

1　单臂壶铃过头推举

1　Single-arm kettlebell press

主要锻炼肌肉

The main exercise muscles

三角肌。

Deltoid.

动作要领

Action tips

身体站直,双脚分开与肩同宽,单手握住壶铃至大臂与肩齐平。双膝略微弯曲,然后迅速蹬地,单臂和双腿互相配合,将壶铃高举过头顶。将壶铃向上推举,并尽可能地保持躯干稳定不动,慢慢地将壶铃放回肩部高度,身体一侧完成所有重复动作后再换另一侧身体。

Stand straightly with your feet shoulder-width apart, lift a kettlebell with one hand to shoulder height. Bend your knees slightly and then quickly pedal, working your arms and legs with each other to lift the kettlebell above your head. Keep your torso as steady as possible while pushing the kettlebell upwards, then slowly lower the kettlebell back down to shoulder height. Once one arm has done all the repetitions, switch to the other.

负荷强度

Intensity

4~6组,每组6~8个。

4-6 groups of 6-8.

图4-2-1 单臂壶铃过头推举

注意事项
Attentions

① 躯干保持直立姿势，运动过程中鼻子和肚脐始终保持在一条直线上，从而确保身体姿势的重心不发生改变。

① Stand up straight, keep the nose and navel are always in a straight line during the process, to ensure that the center of gravity of body posture does not change.

② 在每次重复动作的最低点时肘关节始终位于壶铃的正下方。

② Always keep your elbow directly under the kettlebell at the lowest point of each repetition.

③ 重量不宜过大，向上推举速度越快越好。

③ The weight of kettlebell should not be heavey. The faster the speed of pushing upward, the better the exercise effect.

2 哑铃俯身单臂划船
2 One arm dambbell bent-over row

主要锻炼肌肉

The main exercise muscles

大圆肌、小圆肌、背阔肌和三角肌后束。

Teres major, teres minor, latissimus dorsi and posterior deltoid bundle.

图4-2-2 哑铃俯身单臂划船

动作要领

Action tips

运动员身体呈俯卧姿态，单手支撑在有一定坡度的台阶或者凳子上，另一手紧握壶铃，双臂伸直，躯干成一条直线，单手迅速屈肘提拉自制重物于胸部外侧位置，自然放下，重复以上动作若干次。

The athlete remains in a prone position with one hand supported on a step or stool with some slope, the other hand holding the kettlebell tightly, arms extended and upper torso straight. Quickly bend your elbow with one hand and pull the weight to the outside of your chest, then lower it naturally. Repeat the above movements for several times.

负荷强度
Intensity

8~10 次/组，3~4 组，每组间歇时间 1 分钟。

8-10 times per set for 3-4 sets, 1 minute rest time between each set.

注意事项
Attention

注意控制好身体重心，提拉时身体不要倾斜。

Control the body center of gravity, do not tilt when lifting.

3　壶铃摇摆
3　Kettlebell swing

主要锻炼肌肉
The main exercise muscles

臀大肌、臀中肌、臀小肌和股二头肌。

Gluteus maximus, gluteus medius, gluteus minimus and biceps femoris.

动作要领
Action tips

双脚分开站立，略宽于肩，脚跟脚趾紧抓地面，膝盖朝向脚尖方向，肩膀紧锁，双手握住壶铃，手臂伸直，膝盖微微弯曲，背部保持中立，将壶铃从双腿间前后摆动，利用动力将壶铃甩到身体前面，直到肩膀高度。

Stand with your feet slightly wider than shoulder width apart, gripping the ground with your heels and toes, knees facing towards the toe square. With your shoulders locked, holding the kettlebell in both hands, straight down your arms, bend your knees slightly, and upright the back, swing the kettlebell back and forth from between your legs, throwing the kettlebell in front of your body up to shoulder height.

负荷强度

Intensity

6~8 次/组，4~5 组。

6-8 times per set, 4-5 sets.

注意事项

Attention

① 肩膀始终保持紧锁，壶铃达到最低点时手臂也要伸直。

① Keep your shoulders locked at all times and your arms straight when the kettlebell reaches its lowest point.

② 腿微曲而蹬地发力时，需要顶髋，依靠腿部发力，切忌靠身体摇摆带动壶铃。

② When the leg is slightly bent and the stirrups are fired you need to push your hips and rely on your legs to generate power, don't swing your body to drive the kettlebell.

图4-2-3　壶铃摇摆

第三节　健身球训练方法
Section 3　Fitness ball training methods

1　垂直蹲抛举
1　Vertical squat and throw

主要锻炼肌肉

The main exercise muscles

股二头肌、股四头肌、臀大肌和三角肌。

Biceps femoris, quadriceps femoris, gluteus maximus and deltoid muscle.

图4-3-1　垂直蹲抛举

动作要领

Action tips

双脚分开站立至与肩同宽,将健身球抱至胸前,肘关节位于球体下方。身体下蹲至大腿与地面大致平行,同时躯干挺直,当身体处于最低位置时,伸展双臂并蹬伸双腿,将球垂直向上抛入空中,高度越高越好,不要用手去接球,每次抛出后让它自由落地或等它弹起时,再将球抓住,然后才能开始新一轮练习,重复进行6到10次。

Stand with your feet shoulder width apart and hold the ball to your chest with your elbow under it. Squat down with your thighs are parallel to the floor. When the body is in the lowest position, extend both arms and legs to throw the ball vertically into the air. The higher, the better. Don't catch the ball with your hands. Let it fall freely after each throw and catch the ball when it bounces up. Then start a new round of practice and repeat it for 6 to 10 times.

负荷强度

Intensity

4~6组,每组6~10次。

4-6 sets in all, each set for 6-10 times.

注意事项

Attentions

① 当身体下蹲做每次重复练习时,避免双膝朝身体中线并拢,脚后跟不能离开地面,下肢也应保持紧张。

① As the body squats for each repetition, avoid drawing your knees toward the body midline, and your heels can not leave the ground legs should also maintain tension.

② 每次抛球时,从开始姿势迅速做出动作,同时用力将球扔出,速度越快越好。

② Every time you throw the ball, move quickly from the starting position and throw the ball. The faster, the better.

③ 双脚应离开地面,动作结束时,身体完全打开,双臂举过头顶。

③ Feet should be off the ground and thrown. At the end of the movement, the body should be fully open and the arms should be raised above the head.

2 健身球斜蹲抛举
2 Squat and throw a fitness ball

主要锻炼肌肉
The main exercise muscles
股二头肌、股四头肌、臀大肌和三角肌。
Biceps femoris, quadriceps femoris, gluteus maximus and deltoid muscle.

图4-3-2 健身球斜蹲抛举

动作要领
Action tips
　　双脚分开站立至与肩同宽，将一只重量为3~6公斤的健身球抱在胸前，且肘关节位于球体下方。模仿硬拉的姿势，使身体下压，臀部后移，双膝弯曲，大腿与地面大致平行，同时躯干微微向前倾。在动作最低点时，双臂和腿同时发力，将健身球朝身体斜上方45°角用力抛出,在抛球的同时,你的前倾动作会使你的身体不自主地向前跳,然后走向健身球为下一次重复动作做好准备。

Stand with your feet apart as wide as your shoulder. Hold a 3-6kg fitness ball in front of your chest with your elbow joint under the ball. Imitate the posture of pulling, make the body press down, the buttocks move backward, the knees bend, the thighs are roughly parallel to the ground.At the same time, the trunk leans forward slightly.When the trunkat the lowest point of the action, both arms and legs exert strength.Throw the fitness ball at a 45 degrees angle. When throwing the ball, your body will jump forward involuntarily, and then move towards the fitness ball and get ready for the next repetitions.

注意事项

Attentions

① 每次将球抛出时,身体迅速发力,并且尽可能地用力抛出。

① Each time the ball is thrown, your body works quickly from the start and throw it as hard as possible.

② 每次抛球动作结束时,双脚应该脱离地面,身体完全伸展,且双臂高举过头顶。

② At the end of each throw, your feet should be off the ground, and extend body fully and raise arms above your head.

第四节 弹力带训练方法
Section 4 Training method of resistance band

1 弹力带-腿部练习

1 Elastic band-leg exercise

1.1 弹力带-单腿多方向伸展
1.1 Elastic band – single leg multi direction extension

主要锻炼肌肉

The main exercise muscles

臀大肌、臀中肌和臀小肌。

Gluteus maximus, gluteus medius and gluteus minimus.

图4-4-1 弹力带-单腿多方向伸展

动作要领

Action tips

运动员呈基本运动姿态站立,左脚抬离地面约5厘米,双手叉腰,保持背部挺直,腹部收紧,在运动员膝关节上方套上迷你带,左腿向侧方、后方等多方向快速伸展至最大程度,停顿2秒后收回,换另一侧做以上动作。注意做动作时,始终保持身体平衡和稳定,迷你带处于拉紧状态。为了更深地刺激臀大肌可在踝关节和膝关节同时套上迷你带。

Stand in the basic posture, lift your left foot about 5 centimeters from the ground, rest your arms on the hips, keep your back straight, tighten the abdomen, put on the mini belt above the knee joint of the athlete, quickly extend your left leg to the side, rear and other directions to the maximum extent, stop for 2 seconds and then take back, change the other side to do the above actions. Pay attention to keep your body balance and stability when doing movements, and keep the mini belt tight. In order to stimulate the gluteus maximus more deeply, the mini band can be put on the ankle joint and knee joint at the same time.

负荷强度

Intensity

8~10次/组,3~4组,每组间歇时间30秒。

3-4 sets, each set for 8-10 times, 30 seconds rest time between each set.

注意事项

Attentions

① 锻炼过程中如有疼痛则停止,或者降低强度到无痛为止。

① If there is pain during the exercise, stop or reduce the intensity until there is no pain.

② 使用前,检查弹力带是否存在缺口、裂痕和小孔,防止练习中断裂,弹力带磅数不宜过大。

② Before use, check whether there are gaps, cracks and holes in the elastic band to prevent fracture in practice. The number of pounds of elastic band should not be too large.

③ 避免弹力带与尖锐物或粗糙表面接触，如发现破损应避免使用，弹性下降后需要更换。

③ Avoid contact between elastic belt and sharp objects or rough surface. If damage is found, it should be avoided to use, and it needs to be replaced after elasticity drops.

④ 对橡胶过敏者，应使用不含橡胶的弹力带。

④ If you are allergic for rubber, elastic band without rubber should be used.

⑤ 不要将弹力带过度拉伸，一般不应拉伸至超过原长的3倍。

⑤ Do not over stretch the elastic band. Generally, the length of stretch should not exceed 3 times of the original length.

⑥ 弹力带两端应固定好，以免因松动、脱离而对使用者产生伤害。手握时应环绕手部至少一圈来保证抓握的牢度。

⑥ Both ends of the elastic belt should be fixed to avoid injury to users due to looseness and detachment. Make a circle at least around your hand to ensure firm grip.

1.2 迷你带-横向行走
1.2 Mini belt – lateral walk

主要锻炼肌肉

The main exercise muscles

股二头肌、股四头肌、臀大肌、臀中肌和臀小肌。

Biceps femoris, quadriceps femoris, gluteus maximus, gluteus medius and gluteus minimus.

动作要领

Action tips

运动员呈基本运动姿态站立，双脚左右开立，与肩同宽，双臂微屈，挺直背部，收紧腹部，将迷你带置于膝关节上方，右腿向右蹬地迈出1~2个脚长，左腿蹬地回到起始位置，手臂自然协调摆动。注意始终保持脚尖向前，拉紧迷你带。移动时，重心要稳且始终保持在一个水平面上，两腿不能前后晃动。动作熟练后可在踝关节和膝关节同时套上迷你带，右腿蹬直，左腿跨出较大距离。

The athlete stands in the basic posture, with both feet open to the left and right shoulder width, arms slightly bent, straight back, tight abdomen, place the mini belt above the knee joint right leg pedaling to the right 1-2 feet long, left leg pedaling back to the starting position, arm natural coordination swing. Keep your toes forward at all times and tighten the mini strap. When moving, the center of gravity should be stable and always maintained on a horizontal plane, and the two legs should not sway back and forth. After skillful movement, the mini belt can be put on the ankle joint and knee joint at the same time, and the right leg can be pedaled straight, and the left leg can span a large distance.

图4-4-2 迷你带-横向行走

负荷强度

Intensity

8~10次/组，3~4组，每组间歇时间30秒。

8-10times per set, 3-4 sets, 30 seconds rest time between each set.

注意事项

Attentions

① 锻炼过程如有疼痛则停止，或者降低强度到无痛为止。

① If there is pain during the exercise, stop or reduce the intensity until there is no pain.

② 使用前，检查弹力带是否存在缺口、裂痕和小孔，防止练习中断裂。

② Before use, check whether there are gaps, cracks and small holes in the elastic band to prevent fracture in practice.

③ 避免弹力带与尖锐物或粗糙表面接触，如发现破损应避免使用，弹性下降后需要更换。

③ Avoid contact between elastic belt and sharp objects or rough surface. If damage is found, it should be avoided to use, and it needs to be replaced after elasticity drops.

④ 对橡胶过敏者，应使用不含橡胶的弹力带。

④ If you are allergic for rubber, elastic band without rubber should be used.

⑤ 不要将弹力带过度拉伸，一般拉伸不应超过原长的3倍。

⑤ Do not over stretch the elastic band. Generally, the length of stretch should not exceed 3 times of the original length.

⑥ 弹力带两端应固定好，以免因松动、脱离而对使用者产生伤害。手握时应环绕手部至少一圈来保证抓握的牢度。

⑥ Both ends of the elastic belt should be fixed to avoid injury to users due to looseness and detachment. Make a circle at least around your hand to ensure firm grip.

1.3　迷你带-深蹲

1.3　Mini-belt-squat

主要锻炼肌肉

The main exercise muscles

股二头肌、股四头肌、臀大肌、臀中肌和臀小肌

Biceps femoris, quadriceps femoris, gluteus maximus, gluteus medius and gluteus minimus.

动作要领

Action tips

运动员呈直立姿态正常站位，双脚左右开立，与肩同宽，双手自然放于体侧，保持背部挺直，腹部收紧，双手平举的同时，身体下蹲至大腿与地面平行，保持3~5秒，然后还原呈直立姿态，如此重复若干次。注意下蹲时，膝关节的垂直面尽量不要超过脚尖，脚尖始终保持向前，始终保持好背部平直以及双膝间距。

Stand in an upright position with your feet shoulder-width apart and your hands naturally placed at your sides. Keep your back straight and your abdomen tight. When you raise your hands to the same level as your shoulders, squat down until your thighs are parallel to the ground, hold for 3-5 seconds, then return to an upright position. Make sure that when you squat, the vertical plane of your knees try not to exceed your toes, always keep your toes forward, and always keep your back straight and your knees well-spaced.

图4-4-3 迷你带－深蹲

负荷强度

Intensity

15~20次/组，3~4组，每组间歇时间30秒。

15-20 times per set, 3-4 sets, 30 seconds rest time between each set.

注意事项

Attentions

① 量力而行，深蹲的重量较大，不可盲目增加重量。在缺乏保护与帮助的情况下进行练习时一定要小心谨慎。

① Measure your strength. Because the squat is heavy, do not blindly increase the load. Be careful when performing the exercise without protection or assistance.

② 正确的动作。弓腰塌背练深蹲是错误、危险的。做动作时一定要注意抬头。

② Correct movement. Bowing and collapsing your back while practicing squats is wrong and dangerous. Be sure to keep your head up when performing the movement.

③ 合理的动作节奏。深蹲时切忌速度过快，重心过低，否则极易损伤膝踝等关节。

③ Reasonable rhythm of movement. Do not squat too fast and too low, otherwise it is easy to damage the knees and ankles and other joints.

1.4 迷你带-单腿内收外展
1.4 Mini-belt-abduction and abduction of one leg

主要锻炼肌肉
The main exercise muscles

臀大肌、臀中肌和臀小肌。

Gluteus maximus, gluteus medius and gluteus minimus.

图4-4-4 迷你带-单腿内收外展

动作要领
Action tips

运动员呈基本运动姿态站立,双脚左右开立,与肩同宽,脚尖指向正前方,在运动员膝关节上方套上迷你带,双手叉腰,保持背部与腹部收紧,左腿固定,右腿内收至最大程度,再对抗迷你带阻力使右腿外展至最大程度,如此重复8-10次;换另一侧做以上动作。

Stand in a basic athletic position, with your feet shoulder-width apart and your toes pointing straight ahead.Put a miniband over your knee, cross your arms, and keep your back and abdomen tight, fix your left leg, tuck your right leg in as far as it will go, then against the elastic of the miniband, extend your right leg as far as it will go, repeat 8-10 times; switch to the other side and do the above.

负荷强度
Intensity

8~10次/组,3~4组,每组间歇时间30秒。

8-10 times per set, 3-4 sets, 30 seconds rest time between each set.

注意事项
Attentions

注意保持臀部、腹部收紧,双脚平行,不能离地,脚尖始终向前。

Keep your hips and abdomen tight, stand with your feet parallel to the ground and keep your toes pointed forward at all times.

1.5 迷你带-纵向行走
1.5 Mini-belt-vertical walk

主要锻炼肌肉
The main exercise muscles

股二头肌、股四头肌、臀大肌、臀中肌和臀小肌。

Biceps femoris, quadriceps femoris, gluteus maximus, gluteus medius and gluteus minimus.

图4-4-5 迷你带-纵向横走

动作要领

Action tips

运动员呈基本运动姿态站立,双脚左右开立,与肩同宽,双臂微屈,挺直背部,收紧腹部,在运动员膝关节上方套上迷你带,左脚向前迈步的同时协调摆动手臂,右脚再向前迈出,如此循环。

Stand in a basic athletic position, with your feet shoulder-width apart and slightly bend your arms, straighten your back, tighten your abdomen, put a mini-band over your knees, coordinated your arms swing as you step forward with your left foot, then step forward again with your right foot, and repeat to do the above.

负荷强度

Intensity

8~10次/组,3~4组,每组间歇时间30秒。

8-10 times per set, 3-4 sets, 30 seconds rest time between each set.

注意事项

Attentions

注意做动作时，始终双膝分开，使迷你带拉紧，脚尖指向前方，防止膝关节内扣或者外翻。为了更深地刺激臀大肌，动作熟练后可在踝关节和膝关节同时套上迷你带。

When performing the movement, always keep your knees apart, tighten the mini-band and point your toes forward to prevent the knees from buckling or rolling over. As you become more proficient, the mini-band can be applied to both the ankle and knee for deeper stimulation of the gluteus maximus.

2 弹力带-上肢练习
2 Elastic band – upper limb exercise

2.1 爆发力跪姿俯卧撑
2.1 Kneeling push-ups

主要锻炼肌肉

The main exercise muscles

胸大肌、肱二头肌和肱三头肌。

Pectoralis major muscle, biceps brachii and triceps brachii.

动作要领

Action tips

运动员呈俯撑姿态，双臂距离略宽于肩，双手双膝撑地，手臂伸直，屈肘下沉，身体下落贴近地面时，双手迅速将身体推至空中，然后下落缓冲，继续以上动作。

In a push-up position, keep your arms slightly wider than your shoulders, brace

图 4-4-6　*爆发力跪姿俯卧撑*

your hands and knees on the ground and straighten your arms. Bend your elbows and sink, and as your body drops and close to the ground, push the ground quickly with both hands to get the body off, then sink and cushion, continuing the above movement.

负荷强度
Intensity

8~10次/组，3~4组，每组间歇时间3分钟。

8-10 times per set, 3-4 sets, 3 minutes rest between each set.

注意事项
Attentions

注意在整个过程，应始终保持头、肩、髋、膝、踝成一条直线上，注意保持身体平直，腹部收紧。

Be sure to keep your head, shoulders, hips, knees, and ankles in a straight line throughout the process, keeping your body straight and your abdomen tight.

2.2 弹力带-站姿过顶推举
2.2 Elastic band-standing push

主要锻炼肌肉
The main exercise muscles

三角肌。

Deltoid.

动作要领
Action tips

运动员呈直立姿态，双手屈肘紧握弹力带两端置于肩部上方，双脚踩在弹力带中间位置，与肩同宽，双手用力迅速竖直上推，手臂伸直。使弹力带处于拉紧状态，还原至起始位置，重复以上动作。

In an upright position, bend your elbows and hold the ends of the elastic band above your shoulders, step on the middle of the band with your feet shoulder-width apart. Push it up quickly with both hands, straighten your arms and keep, the elastic band is in a tightened state then return to the starting position, and repeat the above movements.

图4-4-7 弹力带-站姿过顶推举

负荷强度

Intensity

8~10次/组，3~4组，每组间歇时间1分钟。

8-10 times per set, 3-4 sets, 1 minute rest between each set.

注意事项

Attentions

注意挺胸直背，收紧腹部，身体不要晃动。向上推的过程速度要快。

Keep your back straight, your abdomen tight and don't shake your body. The process of pushing up the elastic band should be fast.

2.3 弹力带-俯桥单臂拉
2.3 Elastic band-abdominal bridge single arm pull

主要锻炼肌肉

The main exercise muscles

大圆肌、小圆肌和背阔肌。

Large round muscle, small round muscle and latissimus dorsi muscle.

图4-4-8 弹力带-俯桥单臂拉

动作要领

Action tips

运动员呈俯桥基本姿态，身体呈单臂双脚三点支撑，另一手臂紧握弹力带一端，弹力带另一端固定，利用身体的核心力量和手臂的力量快速拉动弹力带至身体一侧，放回并重复以上动作若干次。

In a basic abdominal bridge position, supporting the body with one arm and two feet and the other arm holding the other end of an elastic band that is secured at one end, using core body strength and arm strength to quickly pull the elastic band to the side of the body, put it back and repeat the above movements several times.

负荷强度

Intensity

8~10次/组，3~4组，每组间歇时间1分钟。

8-10 times per set, 3-4 sets, 1 minute rest between each set.

注意事项

Attentions

保持身体平直，控制好身体姿态。

Keep your body straight and control your posture.

2.4　弹力带-站姿侧平举

2.4　Elastic band-standing lateral lift

主要锻炼肌肉

The main exercise muscles

三角肌前束和三角肌中束。

Anterior deltoid muscle bundle and middle deltoid muscle bundle.

动作要领

Action tips

运动员呈直立姿态站位，双手紧握弹力带两端并置于身体两侧，双脚分开与肩同宽，踩在弹力带中间位置，手肘微屈，双手拉住弹力带迅速向两侧抬起至肩部位置，然后回到起始位置，重复此动作若干次。

In an upright position, hold the ends of the elastic band on both sides of your body, step on the middle of the band with your feet shoulder-width apart. Bend your elbows slightly and pull the elastic band with your hands quickly to your sides until your hands are lifted to the shoulder position and then return to the starting position. Repeat the above movements several times.

图4-4-9 弹力带-站姿侧平举

负荷强度

Intensity

8~10次/组，3~4组，每组间歇时间1分钟。

8-10 times per set, 3-4 sets, 1 minute rest between each set.

注意事项

Attentions

注意保持挺胸收腹，背部挺直，保持身体不要倾斜。

Keep your chest lifted, abdomen tight, back straight and body not tilted.

2.5 弹力带-半蹲直臂拉
2.5 Elastic band–straight–arm pull

主要锻炼肌肉

The main exercise muscles

股二头肌、股四头肌、三角肌前束和三角肌中束。

Biceps femoris, quadriceps femoris, anterior deltoid bundle and middle deltoid bundle.

图4-4-10 弹力带-半蹲直臂拉

动作要领

Action tips

运动员呈半蹲姿态站位，单手紧握弹力带侧平举，手臂伸直，队友双手紧握弹力带站于运动员体侧，拉紧弹力带，运动员直臂迅速将弹力带拉到身体正前方，停顿2秒后还原，重复以上动作若干次。

Stand in a half-squatting position, hold the elastic band with one hand and hold it flat on your side, straighten your arm, a teammate hold the elastic band on your side with both hands and tighten it. Straighten your arm and quickly pull the elastic band directly in front of your body, pause for 2 seconds and then return, repeating the above movements several times.

负荷强度

Intensity

8~10次/组，3~4组，每组间歇时间1分钟。

8-10 times per set, 3-4 sets, 1 minute rest between each set.

注意事项

Attentions

① 注意始终保持腹部收紧，背部挺直，保持身体不要随意转动。

① Pay attention to always keep the abdomen tight, the back straight, keep the body does not turn casually.

② 双手拉紧弹力带至手臂伸直，然后回到起始位置，重复以上动作若干次。注意挺胸收腹，背部挺直，控制好身体重心。

② Be sure to stick out your chest and straighten your back and control your center of gravity.

2.6 弹力带-半蹲姿肩推
2.6 Elastic band – half squat shoulder push

主要锻炼肌肉

The main exercise muscles

三角肌前束、三角肌中束、股二头肌和股四头肌。

Anterior deltoid muscle bundle, middle deltoid muscle bundle, biceps femoris muscle and quadriceps femoris muscle.

动作要领

Action tips

运动员呈半蹲姿态，双手屈肘叉腰，把一根长的弹力带从运动员单侧前胸位置绕到肩部后部（脖子后面）再绕到运动员另一侧前胸位置，保持背部挺直，腹部收紧，弹力带两侧固定在地面上或其他队员用脚踩住，运动员通过蹬地、伸膝、伸髋等动作对抗弹力带迅速向上直立站起,然后回到最初位置,重复以上动作若干次。

In a half-squatting position, bend your elbows with hands akimbo and place a long elastic band from one side of your front chest position around the back of the shoulder (behind the neck) and around the other side of your front chest position, keeping your back straight and your abdomen tight. Both sides of the elastic band are fixed to the ground or stepped on by other players with their feet, the athlete quickly stands upright upward against the band by stirring, extending knees and hips, etc., and returns to the initial position. Return to the original position and repeat it several times.

图4-4-11 弹力带-半蹲姿肩推

负荷强度

Intensity

8~10次/组,3~4组,每组间歇时间1分钟。

8-10 times per set, 3-4 sets, 1 minute rest between each set.

注意事项
Attentions

注意全身协调用力,控制好身体姿态。

Pay attention to the coordinated strength of the whole body, and control your body posture.

2.7 弹力带-半蹲至过顶推举
2.7 Elastic band-half squat to over top push

主要锻炼肌肉

The main exercise muscles

股二头肌、股四头肌、臀大肌、三角肌前束和三角肌中束。

Biceps femoris, quadriceps femoris, gluteus maximus, anterior deltoid bundle and middle deltoid bundle.

图4-4-12 弹力带-半蹲至过顶推举

动作要领：

Action tips：

运动员呈半蹲姿态，双手屈肘紧握弹力带两端置于肩部上方，双脚踩住弹力带中间位置，膝关节不要超过脚尖，蹬地、伸膝、伸髋站起，同时双手拉紧弹力带至手臂伸直，然后回到起始位置，重复以上动作若干次。

In a semi-squatting position, bend your elbows, grip the ends of the elastic band and place them above your shoulders, with your feet in the middle of the band and keep your knees not vance of your toes in the vertical plane. Stomp on the floor, extend your knees and hips and stand up while pulling on the elastic band with both hands until your arms are fully extended, return to the starting position and repeat the above for several times.

负荷强度

Intensity

8~10次/组，3~4组，每组间歇时间1分钟。

8-10 times per set, 3-4 sets, 1 minute rest between each set.

注意事项

Attentions

注意挺胸收腹，背部挺直，控制好身体重心。

Be sure to stick out your chest and straighten your back and control your center of gravity.

2.8 弹力带-硬拉至过顶推举
2.8 Elastic band-dead lift to over top push

主要锻炼肌肉

The main exercise muscles

股二头肌、股四头肌、臀大肌、三角肌前束和三角肌中束。

Biceps femoris, quadriceps femoris, gluteus maximus, anterior deltoid muscle bundle and middle deltoid muscle bundle.

第四章　爆发力训练——单一器械

图4-4-13 弹力带-硬拉至过顶推举

动作要领
Action tips

运动员呈直立姿态，双手紧握弹力带一端于体前，队友紧握弹力带另一端站在运动员体前，此时弹力带处于松弛状态，保持手臂姿态不变，屈髋向后呈俯身姿态，屈膝下蹲至大腿与地面平行，同时支臂拉弹力带至头顶正上方，保持手臂姿态不变，迅速直立站起，然后回到起始位置，重复以上动作若干次。

The athlete is in an upright posture, holding one end of the elastic band in front of the body with both hands, and the other end of the elastic band is standing in front of the athlete. At this time, the elastic band is in a relaxed state. Keep the arm posture unchanged. Bend the hip backward and bend the hip. Squat down until the thigh is parallel to the ground. At the same time, pull the elastic band to the top of the head with the support arm, keep the arm posture unchanged, and quickly stand upright and return to the starting position, repeat the above actions several times.

负荷强度
Intensity

8~10次/组，3~4组，每组间歇时间1分钟。

8-10 times per set, 3-4 sets, 1 minute rest between each set.

注意事项
Attentions

注意俯身时，保持背部挺直，臀部抬高。

When leaning over, keep your back straight and your hips raised.

2.9 弹力带-半跪姿旋转下压
2.9 Elastic band–half-kneeling turnbuckle pull-down

主要锻炼肌肉
The main exercise muscles

腹直肌、腹外斜肌和前锯肌。

Rectus abdominis, external abdominal obliques and anterior serratus muscle.

图4-4-14 弹力带-半跪姿旋转下压

动作要领
Action tips

运动员呈分腿前后跪姿,双手握住弹力带一端至头部侧上方(与前腿同侧),队友紧握弹力带另一端直立站在运动员侧前方,运动员向侧向下方做爆发式转体下拉动作,将弹力带拉至体侧。

Kneel with your legs apart, hold one end of the elastic band to the side of your head (the position of the band is on the same side as the front leg), and your teammate holds the other end of the elastic band tightly, stands straight in front of your side. You should explosively turn your body to pull the band down the side of your body.

负荷强度
Intensity

8~10次/组,3~4组,每组间歇时间1分钟。

8-10 times per set, 3-4 sets, 1 minute rest between each set.

注意事项
Attentions

注意控制好身体的稳定性,前侧腿膝关节不要内扣或者超过脚尖。

Pay attention to control the stability of the body, the knee of the front leg should not buckle inside the toes or over the toes in the vertical plane.

第五节　跳跃训练方法
Section 5　Jumping training methods

1 跳跃爆发力训练

1 Explosive power training

1.1 双腿连续跳
1.1 Continuous jump

主要锻炼肌肉

The main exercise muscles

股二头肌、股四头肌、臀大肌、腓肠肌和比目鱼肌。

Biceps femoris, quadriceps femoris, gluteus maximus, gastrocnemius and soleus.

图4-5-1　双腿连续跳

动作要领
Action tips

运动员呈半蹲姿态，双手屈肘置于身体两侧，做预摆状，身体垂直向上跳起，手臂协调摆动，落地时积极屈髋、屈膝缓冲，然后立刻重复以上动作若干次。

In a half-squatting position, bend your arms and place your hands on either side of your body in a preparatory swing, then jump upward vertically and swing your arms in coordination. When you land, cushion your landing by aggressively flexing your hips and knees, and repeat these movements several times immediately after landing.

负荷强度
Intensity

8～10次/组，3～4组，每组间歇时间3分钟。

8-10 times per set, 3-4 sets, 3 minutes rest for each set.

注意事项
Attentions

① 注意控制好身体重心和注意力的传递。

① Take care to control your center of gravity and pay attention to the delivery of force.

② 跳的距离越远越好。

② Jump as far away as possible.

1.2 立定跳远
1.2 Standing long jump

主要锻炼肌肉
The main exercise muscles

股二头肌、股四头肌和臀大肌。

Biceps femoris, quadriceps femoris and gluteus maximus muscle.

图 4-5-2　立定跳远

动作要领

Action tips

提高下肢动作的力量与爆发力,增强下肢肌肉弹性。运动员原地站好,然后下蹲、手臂后摆,双脚爆发式蹬地向前上方跳起,配合手臂猛烈前摆,在空中展腹、收腿,双腿前伸,落地缓冲。

Improve the strength and explosive power of the lower extremities and strengthen the muscle elasticity of the lower extremities. After standing in place, squat down, swing your arms back, and jump forward and up with your feet exploding on the floor, at the same time, swinging your arms forward, stretch your abdomen and curl your legs in the air, and then stretching your legs forward to cushion when you land.

负荷强度
Intensity

8～10次/组，3～4组，每组间歇时间3分钟。

8-10 times per set, 3-4 sets, 3 minutes rest for each set.

注意事项
Attentions

① 尽量选择平坦且柔软的地面进行练习，如跑道、土地、地板地、沙坑等。过滑的地面不宜练习。

① Choose a flat and soft ground for practice, such as runways, land, floor, sandpit, etc. If the ground is too slippery, you should not practice on it.

② 提高爆发力的练习，重复次数一般不超过10次。提高力量耐力的练习，重复次数必须在10次以上，并尽可能增加重复次数。

② Exercises that can improve explosive power must generally be repeated no more than 10 times. Exercises that can improve strength endurance must be repeated no more than 10 times, with as many repetitions as possible.

③ 落地越轻越好。

③ The lighter the landing, the better.

1.3 单腿侧向跳
1.3 Single leg lateral jump

主要锻炼肌肉
The main exercise muscles

股二头肌、股四头肌和臀大肌。

Biceps femoris, quadriceps femoris and gluteus maximus muscle.

图 4-5-3　单腿侧向跳

动作要领
Action tips

放置五个标志物，两两相隔半米，运动员呈单腿支撑半蹲姿态站于标志物侧方，另一腿略抬起，双手屈肘置于身体两侧，做预摆状，运动员侧向单腿向上跳起连续跳过标志物，手臂协调摆动，落地积极屈髋、屈膝缓冲。

Place five signs, every two half-meter distance apart. Stand at a side of the marker in a squatting posture with one leg supported, raise the other leg slightly, bend your elbows at both sides of the body, do a pre-swing, jump continuously over the marker with one leg facing sideways and upward, swing your arms in coordination, and cushion your landing by actively flexing your hips and knees.

负荷强度
Intensity

8~10次/组，3~4组，每组间歇时间3分钟。

8-10 times per set, 3-4 sets, 3 minutes rest time for each set.

注意事项
Attentions

① 注意控制好身体重心，不要左右晃动。

① Take care to control the body's center of gravity and do not sway your body.

② 一次一次地跳，不要连续，单腿跳得越远越好。

② Jump only once at a time, do not jump continuously. The farther you can jump on one leg, the better.

1.4 后腿高抬单腿连续跳
1.4 Single leg continuous jump with high hind leg

主要锻炼肌肉
The main exercise muscles

股二头肌、股四头肌和臀大肌。

Biceps femoris, quadriceps femoris and gluteus maximus.

图4-5-4　后腿高抬单脚连续跳

动作要领

Action tips

运动员呈前后分腿姿态站位，双脚前后距离适当，以前腿做支撑，后腿抬起脚背置于与小腿等高的台阶或凳子上，下蹲后单腿快速伸髋、伸膝、伸踝向上跳起，跳起在空中时用起跳腿的脚跟触碰臀部，落地屈髋、屈膝缓冲后再立即起跳，重复上述动作若干次。

Stand with your legs forward and backward apart, with the proper distance between your feet. Support by your front leg, raise your back leg and put the back of your foot on a step or stool as high as your calf, squat down and jump up with one leg, extend your hip, knee and ankle quickly, touch your buttocks with the heel of your jumping leg in the air, bend your hip and knee when you land, and jump again immediately after cushioning. Repeat the above movements several times.

负荷强度

Intensity

8~10次/组，3~4组，每组间歇时间3分钟。

8-10 times per set, 3-4 sets, 3 minutes rest time for each set.

注意事项
Attentions
注意控制好身体重心,保持身体的稳定性。
Control the body's center of gravity and maintain body stability.

1.5 单腿半蹲连续跳
1.5 Single leg half squat continuous jump

主要锻炼肌肉
The main exercise muscles
股二头肌、股四头肌和臀大肌。
Biceps femoris, quadriceps femoris and gluteus maximus muscle.

图4-5-5 单腿半蹲连续跳

动作要领
Action tips

运动员呈直立姿态站位，右腿稍离地面，左腿屈膝，双手屈肘做预摆状放于身体两侧，上身保持挺直，左腿迅速蹬地向上跳起，同时双手协调向上摆动，左脚落地缓冲至半蹲姿态后再次重复以上动作若干次。

In an upright posture, slightly raise your right leg off the ground, bend your left leg, bend your elbows and place them on your sides, keeping your upper body straight. Jump up quickly with your left leg, swing your hands upward coordinately, cushion your left foot when it hits the ground, bend it to a half-squatting position and repeat the above actions for several times.

负荷强度
Intensity

8~10次/组，3~4组，每组间歇时间3分钟。

8-10 rtimes per set, 3-4 sets, 3 minutes rest time for each set.

注意事项
Attentions

注意控制好身体重心和身体姿态，落地缓冲时，膝关节尽量不超过脚尖。

Pay attention to the control of the body's center of gravity and posture, when cushioning on the ground, the knee joint should not exceed the toes in the vertical plane.

1.6 弓步交换跳
1.6 Lunges jump

主要锻炼肌肉
The main exercise muscles

股二头肌、股四头肌和臀大肌。

Biceps femoris, quadriceps femoris and gluteus maximus muscle.

图4-5-6　弓步交换跳

动作要领
Action tips
运动员呈弓步姿态站位，双手叉腰，双腿蹬地向上跳起，空中两腿交换，弓步落地缓冲。
Stand in a lunge posture with your hands at your waist, jump up on your legs, exchange your legs in the air once, and land in a lunge posture for cushioning.

负荷强度
Intensity
10～15次/组，3～4组，每组间歇时间1分钟。
10-15 times per set, 3-4 sets, 1 minute rest time for each set.

注意事项
Attentions
注意在起跳和落地过程中保持上体直立，控制身体重心，膝关节尽量不要超过脚尖。
Keep your upper body upright during the jump and landing process, control the

body weight, and try not to exceed the toes of your knees in the horizontal plane.

1.7 抗阻高抬腿跑
1.7 High knees running against resistance

主要锻炼肌肉
The main exercise muscles

股二头肌、股四头肌、臀大肌、比目鱼肌和腓肠肌。

Biceps femoris, quadriceps femoris, gluteus maximus, soleus muscle and gastrocnemius muscle.

图4-5-7 **抗组高抬腿跑**

动作要领

Action tips

运动员呈前后分腿姿态站位，身体前倾，将弹力带置于运动员腰部，队友适当拉紧弹力带，运动员迅速蹬地做高抬腿动作向前跑动。

The athlete stands with legs apart in front and back, leans forward, and wraps the elastic band around the waist. A teammate pulls the band tight behind the athlete with the right amount of force, and the athlete quickly stomps forward to do high leg raises.

负荷强度

Intensity

8~10次/组，3~4组，每组间歇时间3分钟。

8-10 times per set, 3-4 sets, 3 minutes rest time for each set.

注意事项

Attentions

运动时注意手臂协调摆动。大腿抬起高度与地面平行或高于平行面。

Pay attention to the coordinated arm swing during exercise. Thighs should be raised parallel to or above the ground.

第五章 爆发力训练复合器械
Chapter 5　Explosive strength training with instruments

第一节　杠铃类练习
Section 1　Barbell exercises

1　爆发性卧推架杠铃卧推

1　Explosive barbell bench press

动作要领

Action tips

增强上肢的稳定性及爆发力,运动员在卧推凳上呈仰卧姿态,双手比肩略宽握住杠铃,核心收紧,挺胸将杠铃下放至胸部中间,爆发式快起慢落,始终保持肌肉张力。

Enhance the stability and the explosive strength of upper limbs. The athletes are supine on the bench, holding the barbell and hands are slightly wide than shoulders, tightening the core muscles, straightening the chest and putting the barbell to the middle of the chest, explosively fast rise and slowly fall, and always maintain muscle tension.

第五章　爆发力训练复合器械

图5-1-1　爆发性卧推架杠铃卧推

负荷强度

Intensity

选择适宜的重量，在做功速度不减慢的情况下每组8~10次，做4组，每组间歇1分钟。

Select the appropriate weight, 4 sets in all, each set for 8-10 times, then taking 1minute for break. Meanwhile, without slowing down the rate of work.

注意事项

Attention

① 无论做任何训练动作，最初时跟杠铃、哑铃或其他用具的接触是十分重要的，在准备卧推时，先躺在健身椅上，确保你的臀部、腰部、上背及头部都稳稳地放在椅上，双眼要跟杠铃成一直线。

① It is very important to contact the barbell, dumbbell, or other equipment at

131

the beginning of any training action. When preparing for the bench press, lie on the press bench first, make sure that your hips, waist, upper back and head are firmly on the bench, and your eyes should be in line with the barbell.

② 双脚可以放在不同的位置，因为每个人的习惯及生理结构都有所不同，但前提是确保双脚可以透过地面稳稳地发力，不妨试试不同的位置。

② The feet can be placed in different positions, because everyone's habits and physiological structure are different, but the precondition is to ensure that the feet can stably exert force through the ground, and you can try different positions.

③ 握铃距离。

③ The distance of hold barbell.

④ 无论是窄手、阔手或是一般的握法，都能训练胸部，不过由于每个人的生理结构有些许不同，大家可以试试哪种握法最适合你发力。同时，握铃距离也不宜一成不变，中间做出微调，能有效地刺激肌肉。

④ Whether it is short distance, wide distance, or general grip, can strengthen the chest, while, due to everyone's physiological structure is a little different, we can try which grip is most suitable for you. At the same time, the distance of holding the bell should not be fixed, a little change can effectively stimulate muscles.

2 杠铃高翻
2 Barbell high flip

动作要领

Action tips

运动员双脚分开站立与肩同宽，身体浅蹲，挺胸抬头，从地面拉起杠铃。杠铃超过膝盖时，开始爆发性地向上提拉杠铃。稍作停顿，利用硬拉产生向上的惯性，将杠铃拉起到胸部高度，迅速翻转前臂，同时屈髋关节、膝关节，降低重心，将杠铃杆架在肩上锁骨位置。

Athletes stand with feet shoulder-width apart, squat shallowly, keep head up, lift the barbell from the ground. When the barbell is over the knee, lift the barbell explosively. After a short pause, the barbell is pulled up to the height of the chest, turn over the forearm quickly, and flex the hip joint and knee joint, lower the center of gravity, and keep the barbell bar and collarbone at the same height.

图5-1-2 杠铃高翻

负荷强度
Intensity

选择适宜的重量,每组4~5次,做4组,每组间歇1分钟。

Choose the appropriate weight, each set for 4-5 times, 4 sets in all, then taking 1 minute for break.

注意事项
Attention

保持背部挺直,腹部收紧。杠铃向上翻起要快。选择合适的重量,充分热身。

Keep your back straight and your abdomen tight. The barbell should be turned up quickly. Choose the appropriate weight and warm up fully.

3 杠铃高拉
3 Barbell high pull

动作要领
Action tips

运动员站在杠铃后方,双脚间距比臀部略宽,下蹲,双手正握住杠铃,两手握距宽于肩,此时肩膀正好处于杠铃上方,背部呈自然拱形,伸展臀部和膝盖将杠铃拉起,当杠铃拉到差不多膝盖高度的时候,保持杠铃贴近大腿的情况下,猛地抬起肩膀,向上跳将身体伸展开,肘部向两侧打开,将杠铃拉到约颈部的高度,略微弯曲膝盖,将杠铃下放到约大腿中间的位置,在保持下背部收紧的情况下,有控制地缓慢下放杠铃。

Standing behind the barbell, the distance between the feet is slightly wider than that of the buttocks. Squat down and hold the barbell with both hands wider than the shoulder. At this time, the shoulder is just above the barbell, and the back is naturally arched. Extend the hips and knees to pull up the barbell. When the barbell is nearly knee height, keep the barbell close to the thigh, lift the shoulder suddenly and jump up to make body stretch out, open the elbows to both sides, pull the barbell to the height of the neck, slightly bend the knee, lower the barbell to the middle of the thigh, keep the back tight, and slowly lower the barbell.

第五章　爆发力训练复合器械

图5-1-3　杠铃高拉

负荷强度

Intensity

选择适宜的重量，每组4~5次，做4组，每组间歇1分钟。

Choose the appropriate weight, each set for 4-5 times, 4 sets in all, then taking 1 minute for break.

注意事项

Attention

①整个动作过程应该是成一条直线的，杠铃应该尽可能地贴近身体。

①The process of the whole movement should be in a straight line and the barbell should be as close to the body as possible.

②做动作时不要向前倾斜，胸部始终是挺起的。

②Don't lean forward when doing the action, the chest is always up.

③主要的发力点应该来自臀部，不要过分地用上半身的力量来举起杠铃。

③The main starting point should come from the buttocks, do not excessively use the upper part of the body strength to lift the barbell.

④高拉是一个膝盖、臀部、踝关节同时运用到的动作，在你进行高拉之前一定要做好充分的热身。

④High pull is a knee, hip, ankle joint need to be used at the same time, before you start, you must do a full warm-up.

4 颈后杠铃浅蹲

4 Put barbell on the neck and squat

动作要领

Action tips

运动员扛起杠铃，双脚间距略比肩宽，下蹲至大腿与地面平行的四分之一，背部打直与核心收紧，下肢快速地蹬地举起杠铃，在举起杠铃的最后阶段快速提踵，整个过程必须流畅。

Put barbell on the neck. The distance between the legs is slightly wider than the shoulder width. Squat down to a quarter of the thigh parallel to the ground. The back is straight and the core muscles are tightened. The lower limbs quickly push the ground. Raise heel at the last stage of lifting the barbell, the whole process should be smooth.

图5-1-4　颈后杠铃浅蹲

负荷强度

Intensity

选择适宜的重量,每组4~5次,做4组,每组间歇1~2分钟。

Choose the appropriate weight, each set for 4 to 5 times, 4 sets in all, then taking 1 to 2 minutes for break.

注意事项

Attention

① 整个杠铃的活动轨迹从下往上是成一条直线的。

① The whole barbell trajectory is a straight line from bottom to top.

② 脊柱处于中立位,过程核心收紧。

② The spine is in middle position and the core muscles are tightened

③ 踝关节和髋关节活动度差的,可以在脚后跟垫两片小杠铃片。

③ Those people who have poor ankle and hip mobility, can pad two small barbell piece in heel.

第二节 复合器械类
Section 2　Composite instruments

1　快速器械腿伸展

1　Fastly extend leg with instrument

动作要领

Action tips

握住手柄，小腿用力推挤海绵轴，同时双腿伸展，踝关节背屈，直至膝关节完全伸展。进行反向动作，完成一次运动。运动过程中需要移动的配重片不能与其他配重片接触，每次运动接触时它们才能轻微触碰，每次重复运动时都要控制好力度。

Hold the handle, push the sponge shaft with the lower leg, and at the same time, stretch the legs, and dorsiflex the ankle until the knee joint is fully extended. Do a reverse movement so as to complete a set of movement. The counterweight plates that need to be moved in the process of movement can not contact with other. They can only be touched slightly each time when they do the movement. The strength should be controlled well every time the movement is repeated.

图5-2-1　快速器械腿伸展

负荷强度
Intensity

选择适宜的重量,每组8-10次,做4组,每组间歇1分钟。

Choose the appropriate weight, each set for 8-10 times, 4 sets in all, then taking 1 minute for break.

注意事项
Attention

坐姿,挺胸收腹,弯曲膝关节,脚背放在滚板下方,双手握住手柄支撑身体向上慢慢抬起双腿至几乎与地面平行,注意膝关节不要锁死,稍停,收缩股四头肌,慢慢反方向还原。

Sitting posture, straighten your chest and abdomen in, bend the knee joint, put the feet under the rolling board, hold the handle with both hands to support the body, and slowly lift up the legs until they are almost parallel to the ground. Pay attention not to lock the knee joint, stop for a while, contract the quadriceps femoris, and slowly restore in the opposite direction.

2 单手拉力器推举
2 Push the chest expander with one hand

动作要领
Action tips

将拉力器向身体前拉动,左臂模仿划船动作恢复开始姿势,慢慢将手柄收回到身体一侧,同时另一条手臂伸直,肩关节和髋关节都尽量保持不动。后脚伸直,且运动过程中后脚脚跟从地面抬起,躯干稍微前倾,使身体能够移动更大的负荷,每次重复运动之初,肘关节都与身体保持约45度角,为了避免拉力器甩到胳膊,也可以使用弹力带来代替手柄和连接处的这一段绳索。

Pull the chest expander towards the front of the body, the left arm imitate the rowing action and return to the starting position, slowly retract the handle back to one side of the body, and at the same time, straighten the other arm, and keep the shoulder and hip joint still as far as possible. The back foot is straight, and the heel of the hind foot is lifted from the ground during the exercise, and the trunk is slightly tilted forward, so that the body can move more load. At the beginning of each repeated movement, the elbow joint keeps an angle of about 45 degrees with the body. In order to avoid the stretcher throwing to the arm, the elastic band can also be used to replace the rope at the handle and connection.

图5-2-2　单手拉力器推举

负荷强度

Intensity

选择合适的重量，每组6~8次，做4组，每组间歇40秒。

Choose the right weight, do each set of movement for 6-8 times, exercise 4 sets in total, take 40 seconds for break after each set.

注意事项

Attention

一定要始终保持手腕的角度不变，手掌朝向斜上方。

Don't change the angle of your wrist, and maintain your plam being tilted upward.

第六章　爆发力训练测量与评价
Chapter 6　Explosive training measurement and evaluation

第一节　爆发力量测量与评价简介
Section 1　Introduction to explosive force measurement and evaluation

1　爆发力测量评价的意义

1　Significance of explosive power measurement and evaluation

人体所有运动几乎都是为对抗阻力而产生的，所以力量在人体运动中起着至关重要的作用。绝大部分的运动项目，尤其是竞技体育运动，都需要运动员有很强的爆发力。一些项目运动成绩的高低直接与爆发力密切相关。[1]爆发力是力和速度的乘积，是快速大强度运动的基本运动能力。爆发力在克服阻力，使物体产生位移的同时，还能够使物体产生巨大的位移速度。因此，在大多数动力性体育运动项目中，爆发力占据着主导地位，比绝对力量有着更加重要的意义，为提高运动成绩及达到良好的运动效果奠定坚实的基础。爆发力是决定运动成绩的最重要体能要素之一，是投掷、短跑、跳跃及绝大多数非周期性运动项目重要的基本素质，是达到科学训练目的的必备运动能力，同时为正确掌握运动技术和提高运动成绩奠定重要而坚实的基础。

---

[1] 宋全军，聂余满，孙旺强，等.一种用于人体上肢爆发力测试的机器人研究[J].重庆工学院学报（自然科学版），2007（1）：53-56，70.

Almost all human body movements are produced to resist against resistance, so that the power plays a vital role in human body movements. Most sports, especially competitive sports, require athletes to have strong explosive power. The level of some sports performance is directly related to explosive power. Explosive force is the product of force and speed, and is the basic exercise ability for fast and high-intensity exercise. While the explosive force overcomes the resistance and causes the object to produce displacement, it can also cause the object to produce a huge displacement speed. Therefore, in most dynamic sports events, explosive power occupies a dominant position, which is more important than absolute power, and lays a solid foundation for improving sports performance and achieving good sports effects. Explosive power is one of the most important physical factors that determine sports performance. It is an important basic quality for throwing, sprinting, jumping and most non-cyclical sports. It is an essential athletic ability for scientific training purposes, and lay an important and solid foundation for mastering sports skills and improving sports performance.

关于爆发力的测量评价又分为上肢和下肢。因此在各种体育运动项目中，科学的定量测量是训练、诊断及评价肌肉力量应具备的先决条件。目的是为了调控运动员的训练过程以及实现科学的训练计划，从而达到提高运动成绩的训练目标。

The measurement and evaluation of explosive power are divided into upper limbs and lower limbs. Therefore, in various sports, scientific quantitative measurement is a prerequisite for training, diagnosis and evaluation of muscle strength. The purpose is to regulate the athlete's training process and realize the scientific training plan, so as to achieve the training goal of improving sports performance.

对爆发力进行科学的测量与评价，有助于训练信息的及时反馈，以保证训练的科学性和有效性。及时对受训者进行测量与评价是对训练效果的检测，我们在进行爆发力训练时，所面对的训练对象主要分为两类，一是普通大众，二是专业受训者。不管是面对哪类训练对象，在进行爆发力训练时，必须严格遵循以下四个原则：一、效率原则，爆发力训练必须设法以最小的人力、物力、财力、时间达到最大的训练效果。二、特殊原则，爆发力训练必须符合专项运动的特征。三、持续原则，训练期间必须持之以恒，不得间断。四、变动原则，爆发力训练的内容、方式、强度等都要根据受训者的身体状态，相应地进行变动。例如，在进行下肢爆发力训练时可采用：第1阶段无负荷跳跃训练，第2阶段轻负荷跳跃训练，第3阶段重负荷跳跃训练，第4阶段伸展收缩训练。因此，我们进行爆发力的测量与评价时，首先要服务于受测对象。

Scientific measurement and evaluation of explosive power is helpful for timely feedback of training information to ensure the scientificity and effectiveness of training. Timely measurement and evaluation of trainees is a test of training effects. When we conduct explosive power training, the training objects we face are mainly divided into two categories, one is the general public, and the other is professional trainees. No matter what kind of training object you are facing, the following four principles must be strictly followed when conducting explosive power training: First, the principle of efficiency, explosive power training must try to achieve the maximum training effect with the minimum human, material, financial and time. Second, special principles, explosive training must conform to the characteristics of special sports. Third, the principle of continuity, the training period must be persistent and uninterrupted. Fourth, the principle of change, the content, method, and intensity of explosive force training should be changed according to the physical state of the trainee. For example, when performing explosive power training of lower limbs, you can use: the first stage of unloaded jump training, the second stage of light load jump training, the third stage of heavy load jump training, and the fourth stage of stretch and contraction training. Therefore, when we measure and evaluate explosive power, we must first serve the tested object.

2 下肢爆发力的测量与评价
2 Measurement and evaluation of explosive power of lower limbs

下肢力量作为人体力量素质的重要组成部分，对个体下肢进行训练，可以有效地增强跑、跳等运动能力，使全身肌肉力量得到有效地协调发展。下肢力量是反映人体健康的重要指标之一，在运动训练领域，下肢爆发力不仅影响着运动员的运动成绩，还可以作为运动员选材工作时的有效指标。日常生活中，下肢爆发力对个体的活动能力同样具有较大的影响作用，并且还可以作为健康的重要指标，对个体的身体活动进行指导，延缓运动能力的衰退。因此，对下肢爆发力进行测量评价具有较大的现实指导意义，可以有效地促进身体健康的发展，增强自身运动能力。

Lower limb strength is an important part of the strength of the human body. Training the individual's lower limbs can effectively enhance the ability of running and jumping, so that the whole body muscle strength can be effectively developed in a coordinated manner. The strength of the lower limbs is one of the important indicators reflecting human health. In the field of sports training, the explosive power of the lower limbs not only affects the sports performance of the athletes, but also can be used as an effective indicator for the selection of athletes. In daily life, the explosive power of the lower limbs also has a great influence on the individual's activity ability, and can also be used as an important indicator of health, guiding the individual's physical activity and delaying the decline of athletic ability. Therefore, the measurement and evaluation of the explosive power of the lower limbs has great practical guiding significance, which can effectively promote the development of the individual's physical health and enhance their own athletic ability.

3 上肢爆发力的测量与评价
3 Measurement and evaluation of upper limb explosive force

上肢爆发力是人体力量素质的重要组成部分之一。针对人体上肢进行的爆发力训练，可以很好地增强扔、掷、投等运动能力，并且有效地促进整体运动能力发展。上肢爆发力同样也是影响身体健康的指标之一。不仅在专业训练领域广泛地受到人们的重视，在日常的生活中，它对人体综合素质的影响也特别重要。上肢爆发力的测量与评价，对于体操、投掷类、拳击等运动项目具有重要意义，并且对于发展所有项目的综合运动能力至关重要。所以，关于上肢爆发力的测量与评价不管对于大众还是对于运动员都具有重要的意义。

The explosive power of the upper limbs is one of the important components of the human body's strength. Explosive power training for the upper limbs of the human body can well enhance the athletic ability of throwing, throwing, and throwing, and effectively promote the development of overall athletic ability. The explosive power of the upper limbs is also one of the indicators that affects physical health. It is widely valued not only in the field of professional training, but also in daily life, its impact on the overall quality of the human body is also particularly important. The measurement and evaluation of upper limb explosive power is of great significance for gymnastics, throwing, boxing and other sports, and it is very important for the development of comprehensive athletic ability in all sports. Therefore, the measurement and evaluation of the explosive power of upper limbs is of great significance to the public and athletes.

第二节　测量与评价方法
Section 2　Measurement and evaluation methods

1　关于下肢爆发力的测量与评价方法
1　About the measurement and evaluation method of lower limb explosive force

选取了立定跳远、纵跳、原地纵跳摸高三种可反映下肢爆发力的，具有较大代表性的测量方法。

Three measurement methods that can reflect the explosive power of the lower limbs are selected, namely, standing long jump, vertical jump, and in-situ vertical jump.

1.1　立定跳远
1.1　Standing long jump

测量意义：主要反映受试者向前跳跃时下肢肌肉的力量和爆发力。

Measurement significance: It mainly reflects the strength and explosive power of the lower limb muscles when the subjects jump forward.

适用对象：适用于6岁至大学男、女生。

Applicable objects: Suitable for males and females from 6 to university students.

场地器材：立定跳远测量仪、量尺、标志带、平地。

Field equipment: Standing long jump measuring instrument, measuring ruler, marking tape, flat ground.

测量方法：受试者两脚自然分开站立，站在起跳线后，两脚尖不得踩线或过线。两脚原地同时起跳，并尽可能往远处跳，不得有垫步或连跳动作。丈量起跳线后缘至最近着地点后缘的垂直距离。以"厘米"为单位记录成绩，不计小数。测3次，取最佳成绩。

Measurement method: The subject should stand with both feet naturally separated. After standing on the jumper line, the toes should not step on the line or cross the line. Take off with both feet at the same time, and jump as far as possible, without stepping or double jumping. Measure the vertical distance from the trailing edge of the start point of jumper to the trailing edge of the closest point. Record the result in "cm", excluding decimals. Test 3 times and get the best result.

测量要求：

Measurement requirements：

（1）发现受试者犯规时，此次成绩无效。

(1) When the subject is found to be foul, the result will be invalid.

（2）受试者一律穿运动鞋测试，也可以赤脚，但不得穿钉鞋、皮鞋、凉鞋测试。

(2) Subjects will wear sports shoes for the test, and they can also be barefoot, but they are not allowed to wear spiked shoes, leather shoes or sandals for the test.

（3）受试者起跳时不能有助跑或助跳动作。

(3) The subjects cannot perform running or jumping assists when taking off.

评价：立定跳远的测量值越大，则受试者的下肢爆发力就越好。

Evaluation: The greater the measured value of standing long jump, the better the explosive power of the subject's lower limbs.

1.2 纵跳

1.2 Vertical jump

测量意义：主要反映受试者垂直向上跳跃时下肢肌肉快速收缩的能力。

Measurement significance: It mainly reflects the rapid contraction of the lower limb muscles when the subjects jump vertically upwards.

适用对象：适用于6岁至40岁男女。

Applicable objects: Suitable for men and women aged 6 to 40.

测量仪器：电子纵跳计或纵跳计。

Measuring instrument: Electronic vertical jump meter or vertical jump meter.

测试方法：

Test method：

受试者踏上纵跳板，双脚自然分开，呈直立姿势，准备测试，测试时受试者屈膝半蹲，双臂尽力后摆，然后向前上方迅速摆臂，双腿同时发力，尽力垂直向上跳起。当受试者下落至纵跳板后，显示屏显示测试值。以"厘米"为单位记录成绩，精确至0.1厘米。测3次，取最佳成绩。

The subject stepped on the vertical springboard, the feet were naturally separated, in an upright position, ready for the test. During the test, the subject bends the knees and squats, swings the arms as far as possible, and then quickly swings the arms forward and upward, and both legs send simultaneously try to jump up vertically. When the subject fell to the vertical springboard, the display screen showed the test value. Record the result with "cm" as the unit to the nearest 0.1 cm. Test 3 times and get the best result.

测试要求：

Testing requirements：

（1）起跳时，受试者双脚不能移动或有垫步动作。

（1）When taking off, the subject cannot move his feet or has a stepping action.

（2）在起跳后至落地前，受试者不能屈膝、屈髋。

（2）After taking off and before landing, the subject cannot bend knees or hips.

（3）如果受试者没有下落到纵跳板，测试失败，须重新测试。

（3）If the subject does not fall to the vertical springboard, the test fails and must be repeated.

评价：纵跳测量值越大，则受试者下肢爆发力就越好。

Evaluation: The greater the vertical jump measurement, the better the explosive power of the subject's lower limbs.

1.3 原地纵跳摸高
1.3 In-situ vertical jump and touch high

测量意义：主要反映受试者垂直向上跳跃时下肢肌肉快速收缩的能力。
Measurement significance：It mainly reflects the rapid contraction of the lower limb muscles when the subjects jump vertically upwards.

适用对象：适用于6-40岁男女。
Applicable objects：Suitable for men and women aged 6 to 40.

测量器材：纵跳测量板（标有刻度，固定于墙上）、皮尺、白粉末。也可用电子高度计。
Measuring equipment：Vertical jump measuring board (marked with scale and fixed on the wall), measuring tape, white powder. Electronic altimeter can also be used.

测试方法：受试者用右手中指沾些白粉末，身体直立，右侧足靠墙根，右臂上举，身体轻贴墙壁，手伸直，用中指尖在板上点一个指印。测试者先丈量其原地摸高的高度，然后令受试者在离墙20厘米处，用力向上起跳摸高。以"厘米"为单位丈量高度，精确到0.1厘米。测3次，取最佳成绩。
Test method：The subject puts some white powder on the right middle finger, the body stands upright, the right foot is against the wall, the right arm is lifted, the body is lightly against the wall, the hand is straight, and the middle finger is used to make a fingerprint on the board. The tester first measured the height of the in-situ touch, and then asked the subject to jump up and touch the height 20 cm away from the wall. Measure the height with "cm" as the unit, accurate to 0.1 cm. Test 3 times and get the best result.

测试要求：
Testing requirements：

（1）在测验时，起跳和落地均要用双脚，不得跨步、垫步，可做预摆动作。
（1）During the test, both feet must be used for take-off and landing, no

stridding or stepping is allowed, but pre-swing motions can be used.

（2）在原地伸臂点指印时，臂要充分伸直，体侧要轻贴墙壁。

（2）When you stretch your arms in situ to do fingerprints, your arms should be fully extended and your side should be lightly against the wall.

评价：原地纵跳摸高数值越大，则受试者的下肢爆发力越好。

Evaluation: The greater the value of the in-situ vertical jump, the better the explosive power of the subject's lower limbs.

1.4 单脚纵跳测高和单脚纵跳测速
1.4 One-foot vertical jump height measurement and one-foot vertical jump speed measurement

测量意义：主要反映受试者单脚上下垂直跳起的能力。

Measurement significance: It mainly reflects the ability of subjects to jump up and down vertically on one foot.

适用对象：适用于6-40岁男女。

Applicable objects: Suitable for men and women aged 6 to 40.

测量器材：电子纵跳计或纵跳计。

Measuring equipment: Electronic vertical jump meter or vertical jump meter.

测试方法：

Test method:

（1）测高：受试者站在纵跳机踏板上，单脚站立，上身保持直立，准备测试。在听到测试者口令后，半蹲，双臂尽力后摆，然后向前上方迅速摆臂，单腿发力，尽力垂直向上跳起。显示屏显示测试值，受试者需双脚轮流测试。以"厘米"为单位丈量高度，精确到0.1厘米，测3次，取最佳成绩。

（1）Altitude measurement: The subject stands on the pedal of the vertical jumper, stands on one foot, keeps the upper body upright, and prepares for the test. After hearing the tester's command, he squatted halfway, swinging his arms back as far as possible, and then quickly swinging his arms forward and upward, exerting force on one leg, and trying his best to jump up vertically. The display shows the test value, and the test subject needs to take turns to test on both feet. Measure the height with "cm" as the unit, accurate to 0.1 cm, measure 3 times, and take the best result.

（2）测速：准备姿势与单脚测高相同，受试者在听到测试者口令后，以最快的速度单脚屈膝向上跳起，受试者需双脚轮流测试。以"60秒"为单位测量受试者的起跳次数。

（2）Speed measurement: The preparation posture is the same as the one-foot height measurement. After hearing the tester's command, the subject jumps up with one foot bent at the fastest speed. Subjects will be tested on both feet in turn. Take "60s" as the unit to measure the number of jumps of the subject.

测试要求：

Testing requirements:

（1）在测验时，起跳和落地均要用单脚，不得助跑、跨步，可做预摆动作。

（1）During the test, one foot must be used for both take-off and landing, no run-up or stridding, and pre-swing movement.

（2）在做测试前要做好充分的热身活动，以免受试者受伤。

（2）Fully warm-up activities should be done before the test to prevent the subject from being injured.

评价：

Evaluation:

（1）测高：单脚跳高度越大，受试者成绩越好。

（1）Altitude measurement: The greater the one-leg jump, the better the subjects' performance.

（2）测速：一分钟内次数越多，成绩越好。

（2）Speed test: The more times in one minute, the better the results.

2 关于上肢爆发力的测量与评价方法
2 About the measurement and evaluation method of upper limb explosive force

针对上肢爆发力测量的性质,本文主要选取了投掷实心球、快速俯卧撑、快速引体向上,三种可反映上肢爆发力的具有较大代表性的测量方法。

Aiming at the nature of the explosive force measurement of upper limbs, this article mainly selects three representative measurement methods that can reflect the explosive force of upper limbs: Throwing a solid ball, fast push-ups, and fast pull-ups.

2.1 投掷实心球
2.1 Throw a solid ball

测量意义:主要反映受试者上肢肌肉快速收缩克服外界阻力的能力。

Measurement significance: It mainly reflects the ability of subjects' upper limb muscles to quickly contract to overcome external resistance.

适用对象:适用于6-40岁男女。

Applicable objects: Suitable for men and women aged 6 to 40.

场地器材:空旷场地、实心球、卷尺。

Field equipment: Open field, solid ball, tape measure.

测试方法:受试者站在规定投掷线以内,双手持球举过头顶,用力将球向规定区域内投出。测试者丈量实心球第一次落地点到投掷线的距离。以"厘米"为单位丈量距离,精确到0.01米。测试三次,取最好成绩。

Test method: The subject stands within the prescribed throwing line, holds the ball above his head with both hands, and throws the ball into the prescribed area. The tester measures the distance from the first drop of the solid ball to the throwing line. Measure the distance with "cm" as the unit, accurate to 0.01 meters. Test three times and get the best result.

测试要求：测试者测试时双脚不准起跳离地、不准助跑投掷、投掷者身体任何部位不能触碰包括投掷点以外的区域。

Test requirements: During the test, the tester is not allowed to jump off the ground with his feet, not to run and throw, and no part of the thrower's body can touch any area other than the throwing spot.

评价：投掷实心球距离越远，受试者上肢爆发力越大。

Evaluation: The farther the solid ball is thrown, the more explosive power the subject's upper limbsis.

2.2 快速俯卧撑
2.2 Fast push-ups

测量意义：主要反映受试者胸肌、肱三头肌快速克服自身阻力的能力。

Measurement significance: It mainly reflects the ability of the subjects' chest muscles and triceps to quickly overcome their own resistance.

适用对象：适用于6岁至大学生。

Applicable objects: Suitable for students from 6 years old to college.

场地器材：秒表、软垫。

Field equipment: Stopwatch, soft cushion.

测试方法：受试者在软垫上以俯卧撑姿势准备好，测试者手持秒表。受试者听到测试者发出"开始"口令后，快速做俯卧撑。以"1分钟"为单位测量俯卧撑次数。测试一次，记录数据。

Test method: The subject is ready in a push-up position on a soft cushion, and the tester holds a stopwatch. After hearing the tester's "start" command, the subject quickly did push-ups. Measure the number of push-ups in "1 minute". Test once and record the data.

测试要求：测试者测试俯卧撑时，双臂弯曲90度，大臂与地面平行。双腿并拢，不得塌腰。

Test requirements: When testing push-ups, the tester should bend his arms 90 degrees and his arms parallel to the ground. Bring your legs together and don't collapse your waist.

评价：一分钟内次数越多者，上肢爆发力越大。

Evaluation：The more repetitions within one minute, the greater the explosive power of the upper limbs.

2.3 快速引体向上
2.3 Quick pull-ups

测量意义：主要反映受试者背阔肌、肱二头肌快速收缩的能力。

Measurement significance：It mainly reflects the rapid contraction ability of the subjects' latissimus dorsi and biceps.

适用对象：适用于6岁至大学生。

Applicable objects：Suitable for students from 6 years old to college.

场地器材：单杠、保护性软垫、秒表。

Field equipment：Horizontal bar, protective cushion, stopwatch.

测试方法：将准备好的软垫正铺在单杠下，受试者站在单杠下做好准备。测试者手持秒表，发出"开始"口令后，受试者快速上单杠做引体向上。以"秒"为单位测量10秒内引体向上次数。测试一次，记录数据。

Test method：The prepared cushion is being laid under the horizontal bar, and the subject stands under the horizontal bar to prepare. After the tester held a stopwatch and issued the "start" command, the tester quickly went up to the horizontal bar to do pull-ups. Measure the number of pull-ups in 10 seconds in "seconds". Test once and record the data.

测试要求：受试者双脚并立，双手掌心向前，双臂平行正握单杠。向上拉起时，双臂同时用力并确保单杠与肩部齐平。下落时双肘超过90度。

Test requirements：The subject stands with feet side by side, palms forward, arms parallel and holding the horizontal bar. When pulling up, apply force with both arms at the same time and make sure that the horizontal bar is flush with your shoulders. The elbows exceed 90 degrees when falling.

评价：10秒内次数越多者，上肢爆发力越大。

Evaluation：The more repetitions in 10 seconds, the greater the explosive power of the upper limbs.

后记
Postscript

本书采用中英文对照的编写方法，针对以提高身体素质之爆发力的锻炼建立起一套完整训练体系，并创新提出"爆发力量训练+评价量表"的测评模式。教材融可读性、科学性、专业性、知识性、趣味性于一体，也可作为大学生提高自身身体素养的自学读物和锻炼指南。

In this book, a complete training system is established for the training to improve the explosive strength of physical fitness, and the evaluation mode of "explosive strength training + evaluation scale" is innovatively proposed. The textbook integrates readability, scientificity, professionalism, knowledge and interest, and can also be used as a self-study book and exercise guide for college students to improve their physical quality.

自2019年起，我们便构思编写一本适合大学生的爆发力量训练的教材。其一，2016年10月，我国颁布了《"健康中国2030"规划纲要》，第一次把"健康中国"提升为国家战略，明确了建设"健康中国"的思路与任务。2018年教育部体育卫生与艺术教育司司长王登峰表示："2014年全国学生体质健康调研结果显示，全国学生体质健康状况与2010年相比，部分指标有所好转，中小学生身体素质持续下滑趋势在2010年得到初步遏制后，继续呈现'稳中向好'趋势。"其二，大学体育是学校体育与社会体育的衔接点，是大学生健身意识、终身体育习惯和体育能力形成的关键期。由体育意识、体育能力、体育个性、体育品德、体育行为等组成的体育素养，是大学生体育文化修养的重要内容。提升大学生体育素养，增进大学生健康水平，符合"健康中国"和高等教育素质教育的时代要求。其三，人体身体素质中的爆发力，是关乎大学生身体素质的重要环节。爆发力是竞技运动所必需的一种运动素质，但是爆发力训练较少用于普通高校体育教学。其四，结合徒手静力练习，借助杠铃、哑铃、平衡盘、弹力带、瑞士球等器械进行爆发力训练，进行"训练+评价量表"授课测评，可以为不同水平、不同层次的大学生，提供丰富、简单易行、具有参考意义的爆发力训练方法。

Since 2019, we have planned to compile a textbook for explosive strength training for college students. First, in October 2016, China promulgated the planning outline "Healthy China 2030", upgrading "Healthy China" as a national strategy for the first time, and clarifying the ideas and tasks of building "Healthy China". In 2018, Wang Dengfeng, director of the Department of Sports, Health and Art Education of the Ministry of Education, said: "the results of the national student physical health survey in 2014 showed that compared with 2010, some indicators of the national students' physical health improved, and the physical quality of primary and secondary school students continued to decline. After being initially contained in 2010, it continued to show a trend of stable and better." Second, college physical education is the connection point between school sports and social sports, and is the key period for the formation of college students' fitness consciousness, lifelong sports habits and sports ability. Sports quality, which is composed of sports consciousness, sports ability, sports personality, sports morality and sports behavior, is an important content of college students' sports culture. It is in line with the era requirements of "Healthy China" and quality education of higher education to improve college students' sports literacy and health level. Thirdly, the explosive strength in human body quality is an important link related to college students' physical quality. Explosive strength is a necessary quality of competitive sports, but explosive strength training is rarely used in college physical education. Fourth, combined with the unarmed static exercise, with the help of barbell, dumbbell, balance plate, elastic band, Swiss ball and other equipment for explosive strength training, the "training + evaluation scale" teaching evaluation, can provide abundant, simple and referential explosive strength training methods for college students of different levels.

2019年9月，我们组成由申军辉、张亚坤、高昊、达志强、熊一鸣、马力强、王绥隆、张兴涵等同学参与的编写小组。在编写过程中，参考和借鉴大量文献和最新成果，特别是顾德明先生的运动解剖学图谱。由兴趣入手，结合大学生的身体特点,选取运动解剖学图谱,插入锻炼小帖士,制订评价量表,以深入浅出的语言,图文并茂的形式,由浅入深、由易到难递进式,给出促进针对不同肌肉的爆发力量训练方法。

In September 2019, we formed a compilation group with the participation of Shen Junhui, Zhang Yakun, Gao Hao, Da Zhiqiang, Xiong Yiming, Ma Liqiang, Wang suilong, Zhang Xinghan and other students. In the process of compiling, a large number of literatures and the latest achievements, especially Mr. Gu Deming's Atlas of sports anatomy, were used for reference. Starting from the interest, combined with the physical characteristics of college students, selected the exercise anatomy atlas, with the exercise tips inserted, and the evaluation scale formulated, in the form of simple language and photo-illustrated, the method of promoting the training of different muscle explosive strength is given.

2020年6月,初稿完成,邀请动作模特董姝含、高昊进行教学技术动手示范与拍摄,并由聂世轩、张亚坤、王绥隆、张兴涵、陈永欢和尚远对全书进行英文翻译。2020年9月,我们对全书进行最后的修改与校对。2020年10月1日,《爆发力训练》最终定稿。

In June 2020, the first draft was completed, and action models Dong Shuhan and Gao Hao were invited to conduct demonstration and shooting of teaching technology. Nie Shixuan, Zhang Yakun, Wang suilong, Zhang Xinghan, Chen yonghuan and Shangyuan translated the book into English. In September 2020, we make the final revision and proofreading of the book. On October 1, 2020, "explosive strength training" was finalized.

值此付梓之际,感谢人民体育出版社领导及相关编辑,感谢学校相关部门、学院领导与同事,感谢本书所参考的中外优质文献作者,同时也要感谢我的研究生团队鼎助。尽管团队在本书的编写过程中竭力付出,难免有遗憾与不足。由于时间仓促,且待将来完善充实。书中若有不妥之处,敬请广大读者批评指正。

On the occasion of publication, we would like to thank the leaders and editors of the People's Sports Publishing House, leaders and colleagues of the relevant departments and colleges, the high-quality literature authors at home and abroad referred in this book, as well as my graduate team for their help. Although the team in the process of writing this book to pay, there are inevitably regrets and deficiencies. Due to the lack of time, it may be improved in the future. If there is something wrong in this book, please criticize and correct it.

黄迎乒，张振东于郑州大学

2020年11月9日

Huang Yingping, Zhang Zhendong in Zhengzhou University

November 9, 2020